Carmen Bin Ladin lives in Switzerland with her three daughters.

THE VEILED KINGDOM

On September 11th 2001, Carmen Bin Ladin heard the news that the Twin Towers had been struck. She instinctively knew that her brother-in-law's name would be linked to these horrifying acts of terrorism, and her heart went out to the victims in America. She also knew that her life and the lives of her family would never be the same again. In 1974, Carmen — half Swiss and half Persian — married Yeslam Bin Ladin and found herself part of a culture that she neither knew nor understood. Her story takes us inside one of the most powerful, secretive and repressive kingdoms in the world and the Bin Laden[1] family's role within it.

---

[1] In accordance with convention, the spelling Bin Laden is used when referring to the clan and its members, and Bin Ladin when referring to Yeslam and Carmen.

CARMEN BIN LADIN

◆

THE
VEILED
KINGDOM

Complete and Unabridged

ULVERSCROFT
Leicester

First published in Great Britain in 2004 by
Virago Press
an imprint of
Time Warner Book Group UK
London

First Large Print Edition
published 2005
by arrangement with
Time Warner Book Group UK
London

The moral right of the author has been asserted

All photographs are from the author's private collection

British Library CIP Data

Bin Ladin, Carmen
    The veiled kingdom.—Large print ed.—
Ulverscroft large print series: non-fiction
    1. Bin Ladin, Carmen—Family 2. Bin Laden (Family)
    3. Women—Saudi Arabia—Biography
    4. Large type books 5. Saudi Arabia—Social life and
customs—20th century
    I. Title
    953.8'053'092

    ISBN 1–84395–811–2

Published by
F. A. Thorpe (Publishing)
Anstey, Leicestershire

Set by Words & Graphics Ltd.
Anstey, Leicestershire
Printed and bound in Great Britain by
T. J. International Ltd., Padstow, Cornwall
This book is printed on acid-free paper

Acknowledgements

I would like to express my deepest gratitude and love to:

My daughters, Wafah, Najia and Noor, for their immeasurable courage and the strength and support they have shown me during those long years of struggle. In spite of the dark times that they have lived through, they have managed to become beautiful human beings.

My mother, who always made me feel loved and special and whose courage has inspired me.

Mary Martha Barkley, who is always there for me. My life would have been much the poorer without her example.

Thomas, who lavishes love and unconditional support on my daughters.

Frédéric Marti, whose understanding, talent and tenacity have enabled me to keep my girls.

Peter Lilley, who believed in me from our very first meeting.

Pierre Alain Schmidt, who has had the courage to defend me in my divorce case and to stand by me even when it seemed hopeless.

Working on this project has allowed me to meet two fantastic people, Susanna Lea and Ruth Marshall, whose patience and support have been invaluable. I know they will be part of my life for ever.

And of course, I would like to express my special love and thanks to my friends, who have been there for me at even the most difficult times: Sabine and Matthias Kalina, Lois, John and Shelton West, Ula Sabag, Géraldine, Ulrika, Carlos and Guillaume.

Contents

Note: All the events in this book happened as I described them. However, I have changed the names of two dear friends, Latifa and Turki, at their request, as well as the name of Latifa's father.

Preface

A Letter to My Daughters

My dearest Wafah, Najia and Noor,

It is with great joy and hope — and also some apprehension — that I undertake the task of writing the story of my life. This book is for you. Of course, you will already have heard some of my stories, and are vaguely aware of the Saudi way of life, but I hope that this will enable you to comprehend the part of your background that you, Wafah and Najia, have completely forgotten and that you, Noor, have never known. Over the years, watching you grow into the beautiful human beings that you are, I came to feel that an insight into my personal experiences of living in Saudi Arabia would also give you a better understanding of the difficult times that you have had to go through since we left that country.

As you know, it is my utmost conviction that freedom of thought and expression is the most valuable gift of all. I want you never to take that freedom for granted. I

1

want to reaffirm what you already know: that although material wealth may give pleasure, it is meaningless when it exists in a golden cage — especially when, as a woman, you cannot do what you want or be who you want to be.

Although, for obvious reasons, I have not returned to Saudi Arabia in recent years, I continue to discuss events there with my friends inside the Kingdom. I can see that their lives have not evolved. Deep down in my heart, I am convinced that my decision to raise you with Western values was the right one, even if the effect has been to sever ties with that country. The only regret that I have — and always will have — is the emotional price that you have paid. I hope it is a consolation to you that I feel honoured and privileged to be your mother. Without you I know that I would be a far lesser person: you are the source of my courage, my strength, my will.

Above all, I want you to know that any steps that I have taken — whether they were right or wrong — were born out of my love for you. Thank you for what you have given me, by being yourselves. By being you.

1

Nine Eleven

September 11 2001 was one of the most tragic dates of our lifetime. It took, and shattered, the lives of thousands of innocent people. It robbed the world of its sense of freedom and security. It was a nightmare of grief and horror — one which I, and my three daughters, will never forget.

And yet Nine Eleven began as a lovely Indian summer's day. I was enjoying a leisurely drive from Lausanne to Geneva with my eldest daughter, Wafah, when one of my closest friends, who was working in New York, called me on my cell phone.

'Something terrible just happened,' he said, his voice urgent, from his office just a few blocks away from the attack. 'It's incredible. A plane hit one of the towers of the World Trade Center.' And then, his voice rising further, he yelled, 'Wait a minute. There's another plane. It's going straight towards the second tower. Oh my God,' and he was screaming now, 'It hit the second tower!' As

3

he described the second hit, something in me snapped. This was no freak accident. This had to be a deliberately plotted attack on a country I had always loved and looked on as my second home. I froze. Then waves of horror crashed over me as I realized that somewhere at the bottom of this lay the shadow of my brother in law: Osama Bin Laden.[1]

Beside me in the car, Wafah was yelling, 'What? What happened?' I was in shock. I managed to force out a few words. Wafah lived in New York. She had just graduated from Columbia Law School, and had spent the summer with me in Switzerland. She was planning to head back to her apartment in four days' time. Now she was in tears, clicking frantically on her cell phone, trying to reach all her friends. My first instinct was to call my dearest friend, Mary Martha, in California. I had to hear her voice. She had already heard about the double attack in New York, and she told me a third plane had just hit the Pentagon. The world was spinning off

---

[1] Western transliterations of Arab names vary considerably. In accordance with convention, the spelling 'Bin Laden' is used when referring to the clan and its members, and 'Bin Ladin' when referring specifically to Yeslam and Carmen.

4

its axis; I could feel it.

I raced to the high school attended by my youngest daughter Noor. The look of shock in her eyes told me she already knew. The blood had drained from her face. We rushed home to meet my middle girl, Najia, as she returned from college. She, too, was devastated. Like many millions of other people around the world, we watched CNN, mesmerized, alternately weeping and phoning everyone we knew.

As the hours passed, my worst fear came true. One man's face and name was on every news bulletin: Osama Bin Laden. My daughters' uncle. A man whose name they shared, but whom they had never met, and whose values were totally foreign to them. I felt a sick sense of doom. This day would change all of our lives, for ever.

★ ★ ★

Osama Bin Laden is the younger brother of my husband, Yeslam. He is one of many brothers, and I knew him only distantly when I lived in Saudi Arabia, years ago. At the time, Osama was a young man, but he always had a commanding presence. He was tall and stern, and his fierce piety was intimidating, even to the more religious members of his family.

During the years that I lived among the Bin Laden family in Saudi Arabia, Osama came to exemplify everything that repelled me in that opaque and harsh country: the unbending dogma that ruled all our lives, the arrogance and pridefulness of the Saudis and their lack of compassion for people who didn't share their beliefs. That contempt for outsiders and unyielding orthodoxy spurred me on to a fourteen-year fight to give my children a life in the free world.

In my struggle to sever our ties to Saudi Arabia, I began amassing information on my husband's family. I watched as Osama grew in might and notoriety, spiralling deeper into murderous rage against the United States from his redoubt in Afghanistan. Osama was a warlord who assisted the Afghan rebels in their fight against the Soviet occupation of their country. When the Soviets left, Osama returned home, and for many he was already a hero.

When Iraq invaded Kuwait in 1990, Osama was outraged at the idea that US forces might use Saudi Arabia as a base. He offered King Fahd the use of his Afghan warriors to fight against Saddam Hussein. Some of the more religious princes thought Osama's ideas had merit, but King Fahd refused. Osama began making incendiary statements against the corruption and moral bankruptcy of the Saudi ruling family, and the Americans who were defending them. Finally, he was forced to leave the country and take refuge in Sudan, where his compound of armed men was surrounded by sentries in tanks. Then he moved back to Afghanistan.

In those days, even though we were separated, I was still on speaking terms with Yeslam who kept me up to date with developments in Saudi Arabia and the Bin Laden family news — including Osama's whereabouts. Yeslam told me that Osama's power was growing, despite his exile. Osama, he said, was under the protection of an extremely powerful, conservative and highly respected prince. He even told me who he was.

In 1996, when a truck bomb blasted the Khobar Towers living quarters of American forces posted in Dahran, in eastern Saudi Arabia, Osama was mentioned as a possible culprit. I was dumbstruck, yet I knew it could be true. Who else could have at his disposal enough explosives in a country so highly controlled? Osama was a warrior, a zealot, and a member of the family that jointly owned the Bin Laden Organization — the wealthiest and most powerful construction company in Saudi Arabia. I knew of Osama's fiercely extreme opinions, and deep down I felt that he was capable of a terrible, blind violence.

As attack followed attack, I read everything I could lay my hands on about Osama. So, on 9 September 2001, when the news broke of the attack on the Afghan fighter Ahmed Shah Massoud, I realized it had to be Osama's doing. I walked over to the television, with a sick feeling of fear in my stomach. 'This is Osama. He is getting ready for something truly awful.' 'Oh, Carmen, you're obsessed,' scoffed a friend of mine. But I knew. I wish I had been wrong.

It never occurred to me that Osama was plotting an assault on the heart of New York. I thought perhaps it would be an embassy — that would have been bad enough. But when the World Trade Center went down in flames just two days after Massoud's death, the fear hit me again, and I know that it will never go away.

In the days that followed the attack on the World Trade Center, our lives revolved around the TV news bulletins. The toll of victims kept rising as the dust settled on the ashen streets of my children's favourite city. We watched people searching for the missing, clutching old snapshots in their hands. Bereaved relatives told reporters about the last phone messages left on their answering machines before their loved ones died. There were those awful photographs of people jumping. I kept thinking, 'What if Wafah had been there?' I felt so very deeply for those mothers, for those children.

My three girls were distraught with grief and bewilderment. Noor, who, just one year earlier, had brought an American flag home from South Carolina to stick on her bedroom wall, sank into despondency. She sobbed, 'Mum, New York will never be the same.' Fortunately, she never became the target of hostility from her classmates: her pro-American cheerleading had made her the subject of friendly teasing for years, so all her friends realized how truly hurt my little girl was.

We hardly left the house. Reporters called constantly as I was the only Bin Laden in Europe with a listed phone number. Friends called, their voices strained. Then they stopped. We were rapidly becoming personae non gratae. The Bin Laden name frightened even the hardiest professionals. A new law firm refused to take on my divorce case and I suddenly found myself without a lawyer.

Of all of us, it was Najia who focused most on the suffering of the World Trade Center's victims. Most of the time she could hardly watch TV. Her name was becoming public currency: this was particularly hard to bear for such a private person. Najia is perhaps the most discreet of all my children. She doesn't display her emotions easily, but I could see she was stricken.

The terrible irony was that we identified, and grieved with, the victims, while the outside world saw us as the aggressors. We were trapped in a Kafkaesque situation, particularly Wafah. After four years of law school, Wafah's life was in New York. Her apartment was just blocks from the World Trade Center. She talked night and day about her friends there. She felt she had to be there, and wanted to fly back immediately.

Then one newspaper reported that Wafah had been tipped off and had fled New York just days before the attack. This was untrue. Wafah had been with me, in Switzerland, since June. But other papers picked up the story and repeated that Wafah had known about the attack in advance, and had done nothing to protect the people and the home that she loved. A friend who was staying in Wafah's apartment called to say that she had begun receiving death threats. It was an understandable reaction — how could strangers distinguish one Bin Laden from another?

I felt I had no choice. Only I could defend

my daughters. I issued a statement saying that my three girls and I had had no connection whatsoever with this evil, barbaric attack on America — a country we loved and whose values we shared and admired. I went on TV and I wrote to the newspapers to express our sorrow. My long battle to free myself and my children from Saudi Arabia was all the evidence I could offer for our innocence: that, and our good will and the pain we felt for Osama's victims.

I had so longed for an end to my bitter fight against the Bin Ladens and their country, but now I faced a whole new struggle. I would have to shepherd my children through the anguish they felt as their name became synonymous with evil, infamy and death. My private life had become a public story.

★ ★ ★

Ironically, it was only after Nine Eleven that my fourteen-year fight for freedom from Saudi Arabia made sense to the people around me. Before that, I think no one truly understood what was at stake — not the courts, not the judge, not even my friends. Even in my own country, Switzerland, I was perceived, more or less, as just another woman embroiled in a nasty international divorce.

But I always knew that my fight went far deeper than that. I was fighting to gain freedom from one of the most powerful societies and families in the world, to salvage my daughters from a merciless culture that denied them their most basic rights. In Saudi Arabia they could not even walk alone in the street, let alone choose the path of their own lives. I fought to free them from the hard-core fundamentalist values of that society and its contempt for the tolerance and liberty of the West, which I have learned to value deeply.

I am afraid that even today the West does not fully understand Saudi Arabia and its rigid value system. For nine years, I lived inside the powerful Bin Laden clan, with its close and complex links to the royal family. My daughters went to Saudi schools and I lived, to a great extent, the life of a Saudi woman. And over time, I learned and analysed the mechanisms of that opaque society, and the harsh and bitter rules that it enforces on its daughters.

I could not stand quietly by while my little girls' bright minds were suppressed. I could not teach them to submit to the values of Saudi culture. I could not watch them be branded as rebels because of the Western values that I taught them — with all the punishment that might ensue. And were they to comply with Saudi society's rules, I could not face the prospect that my daughters might grow up to become like the faceless, voiceless women I lived among.

Above all, I could not watch my daughters be denied what I valued most: freedom of choice. I had to free them, and myself.

This is my story.

2

A Secret Garden

There was a carefree feeling in the air the year I met my husband Yeslam. It was 1973 and young people ruled the world. I was outgoing and sociable, a couple of years out of high school but I felt a little lost that summer as I looked around me for the path I wanted my life to take. I wanted to study law so I could defend the defenseless. I wanted to travel and have adventures. I also wanted to give my life a sense of meaning, but my mother, who came from an aristocratic Persian family, was bent on my getting safely married.

My three sisters and I would often crowd into one of our bedrooms, in my mother's house outside Geneva, and listen to Beatles LPs, talking about our future. I was the eldest and I suppose I talked the most. I always insisted, in those days, that I would never marry a Middle Easterner, as my mother would have liked. I was attracted to the freer lives of the Americans I had seen as a little girl at the American Club near my great-aunt's house in Iran. Their lives seemed brave, modern and free. They drove jeeps, wore jeans and ate hamburgers, whereas people from the Middle East lived lives that seemed so closed off, hobbled by layers of tradition and secrecy, where appearances seemed more important than desires.

I was born in Lausanne, to a Swiss father and a Persian mother. My mother's family, the Sheibanys, was cultivated and aristocratic. When I was little, my mother took us to Iran for long vacations every year or so. I loved Iran: the spicy food, so subtle and aromatic; what seemed like acres of roses tended by invisible gardeners in my grandmother's high-walled garden; and the grand old house where my mother had grown up, with its blue-tiled steam-room dim with vapour; the huge library of ancient books, the lattice-work shutters, the richly coloured carpets and fine antiques. I thought Iran was a special country — high in colour and drama. I loved the months we spent there. My grandmother treated me like a little princess. I adored her and I knew she adored me.

When I was seven or eight, my mother gave a party in my grandmother's house. The rooms were filled with people she had grown up with: well-known writers and intellectuals

15

from old families, who shared my grandmother's aristocratic scorn for the parvenu Shah. Their discussions were way above my head, but the atmosphere was exciting. When the time came to go to bed, I refused point-blank to go upstairs to my room.

'Daddy is coming,' I kept insisting, though my mother told me again and again that he was in Switzerland, hard at work. I wore my mother's patience to shreds that night. Then, just as I was about to give up and go to bed, my beloved father walked through the door. He hadn't phoned ahead, he had just impulsively taken an aeroplane. I was overjoyed, and, wickedly, triumphant.

When my grandmother realized that there truly was no way I could possibly have known in advance of my father's arrival, she bent over and held me at arm's length as she looked in my eyes. 'Carmen,' she said, 'you are a very special person. Never forget that.' Every child should feel the way I felt that night.

My grandmother had a swimming pool, and my handsome, charming father used to dive straight into it from the upper floor, to our squeals of horror and delight. One day my little sister Béatrice, a toddler, fell in, and my mother, decked out in an elaborate pink silk dress with a tight waist and wide skirt, leapt into the pool to save her. Her skirt puffed out hugely, like a parachute. To this day I can see my mother emerging with Béatrice in her arms, fully clothed, water streaming from her dress, but nonetheless still beautiful.

I was a curious child, and like many children I could sense the importance of adult conversations, even when the details were far beyond my understanding. I loved to listen in on political discussions. As far back as I can remember, all my life I have sought to analyse things around me, even when they seem far beyond my reach.

When I was about seven, my grandmother's household went into terrible turmoil when a cousin of my mother's, Abbas, was arrested and tortured by the Shah's fearsome SAVAK secret police. They claimed he was a member of the Communist Tudeh party. That summer, the big song on the radio was 'Marabebous'. It was about a man who is sentenced to death, asking his daughter to kiss him for the last time. I used to play it again and again, full of sorrow. I wanted to know why that man had to die, and I wondered if my mother's cousin would have to die too. What had he done? I suppose this was the first time I realized that someone could pay for their beliefs with their life.

Iran was my secret garden, something that made me different from the other little Swiss girls in our local school outside Lausanne. But when I was nine, my mother suddenly cut off all connection with Iran. My father had left her, and she didn't want to admit it. If she acknowledged that her marriage had failed, she would lose face with her relatives. So, rather than tell the truth, she withdrew from any close contact with her own family.

For a long time my mother didn't even tell us, her four daughters, that she and my father were separating. She told us he was away on business, but my instinct told me otherwise. I knew that this was the way my mother lived — if something was disagreeable, you evaded it, denied it or suppressed it. If you never spoke of it, it didn't exist. What counted was saving face.

After my father left, my mother brought us up with the help of a governess. For years I had no contact with my father at all, and nobody explained why. I learned not to ask. I realized early on that I must live between two cultures, caught somewhere between the Iran that had shaped my mother's strict rules of behaviour, and the local Swiss school I attended. Home was a strange, silent space where everything important was unspoken.

I knew that my mother was born a Muslim

18

because her father had been one, and, in Islam, you adopt your father's beliefs. But my mother wore her Islam lightly and didn't practise it in any formal sense. I saw her pray a handful of times, but not in the traditional sense of bowing and kneeling, and facing Mecca. If she wanted to pray, she might just as easily enter a church as a mosque. She didn't fast during the Ramadan month, or wear a headscarf. I saw my grandmother veiled occasionally, when she had sheep killed and distributed as alms to the poor. Being a Muslim seemed natural if you were from the Middle East, but it didn't enforce any regimented lifestyle on my mother or on us children.

It was my mother's sense of propriety that restricted our lives as normal Swiss girls. There was no rough play or rumpled clothes, no late night parties or dates, but like all teenagers, we learned to circumvent those strict rules. We weren't angels and she never locked us in. Although it was important to her that we continue our studies, marriage was her ultimate goal for us, and she tried to direct every detail of our lives. Until I was older and openly rebelled, our mother dressed the four of us exactly alike, down to the ribbons in our plaits. 'You can be perfectly elegant, but if you have a single stain you are nothing,' she would say. For my mother, decorum was vital.

When I was an adult, one of my mother's cousins told me the story of my parents' marriage. My mother had come to Lausanne to study and had met my father. They eloped to Paris and came back married, and there was nothing her family could do about it. This was the kind of person she was underneath: impetuous and rebellious, the kind of woman who would name her daughters Carmen, Salomé, Béatrice and Magnolia. My mother left her country, eloped with the man of her choice and drove a car. Strangely, in a sense, my mother was a pioneer.

But later she suppressed that personality, maybe because her marriage had failed. As we grew up, my mother seemed to care only about what other people would think. She insisted on bringing up her children within something like the conventions that she herself had sought to flee. She couldn't admit that my father had left her for someone else, because if her marriage had failed, that would prove to her own mother that her elopement had been wrong.

That was what it meant to me, to be from the Middle East. You lived behind secrets. You hid things that were disagreeable. You had to submit to the conventions of society. Saving face could justify dishonesty. Only appearance mattered. My personality was different. To me, truth was important, and I didn't like to submit. Instead of bending to my mother's rules, I began confronting her, defiantly. I remember telling her to stop pushing me into situations where I would have to lie to her. I wanted to force her to accept the reality of my character.

In high school, both my sister Salomé and I started to smoke. My mother offered to buy us anything we wanted if we gave up our cigarettes. Salomé wanted a car, so my mother bought her a Fiat, but Salomé kept on smoking, in secret. My mother took me to a furrier's to try on a leopard-skin coat. She told me, 'Promise me that you will never smoke another cigarette and I will buy it, right now, today.' I wanted to — I wanted that coat — but I didn't want to make a promise that I knew I could not keep.

As I grew into adulthood, I found myself in moral turmoil, handicapped by the contradictions of my upbringing and personality. I lived in the West. I was impetuous and impulsive. I longed to be free, but so much of my background lay in the conventions of Middle Eastern culture, where clan rules are more important than personality. In the

Middle East, you never develop as an individual. People may manage to escape their traditions for a short while, but then those rules eventually catch up with them.

I knew I should decide for myself what path my life should take, but I was too inexperienced and mixed up to do it alone. I was waiting for help — for some sort of sign.

3

Falling in Love

The first time I met Yeslam, I had no idea that this man would change my life for ever. It was the spring, and Geneva was full of Saudi Arabian tourists. My sisters and I were planning a vacation to visit my grandmother in Iran, so my mother had agreed to rent out one floor of her house for the summer to a Saudi Arabian family. This slight young Saudi man, dressed in black from head to toe, had come to finalize the agreement. I glanced at him and he smiled politely. Then my grandmother injured her leg and our trip to Iran was cancelled. It was too late to call off the rental, so my sisters and I shuttled between an apartment in Lausanne and my mother's house, where she hosted her Saudi guests.

Yeslam's mother was Iranian like mine. She was a soft-spoken woman with a sweet, round face and darkly dyed hair. She wore long dresses and a simple Muslim head-covering. We spoke in Persian. Yeslam's younger brothers, Ibrahim and Khalil, had wild Afros and platform shoes. Fawzia, the younger sister, looked like any European teenager with tight T-shirts, long wavy hair and big tinted sunglasses. And then there was Yeslam.

Yeslam intrigued me. He was calm, but he had a compelling authority. He was slim, bronzed and handsome. He didn't speak much, but his eyes were penetrating and gentle. And mostly they looked at me. Slowly, we began talking in English together and simple chit-chat evolved into long conversations. As time passed, Yeslam became increasingly attentive. He began insisting that I accompany him and his family on their trips around town. Yeslam was crazy about his two Dobermanns. He was twenty-four years old, a little older than me and my friends, and different. He acted like a grown-up. As his mother's eldest son, Yeslam was the head of the family, and did as he pleased. He was responsible and leadership seemed to come naturally to him. For everybody, even his mother, his brothers and sisters, Yeslam's word was law. Even my mother started to look to him for direction.

I can see now that Yeslam's natural authority came from the Saudi culture in which he grew up, where the eldest son commands every gesture of his clan. Then, though, I saw only a man who was courting me, who was exotic and beautiful, and whose company I came to find fascinating. Yeslam was clear-sighted. He had a sharp mind and a strong will. He remembered every detail of anything I said. He understood me. He seemed to need me, and I began to feel that I was the only person in the world in whom he could confide. There was no moment when I could say that I suddenly fell for him, but I had fallen in love.

As the summer passed, Yeslam and I began to look for each other every day. We spent every free moment together. I had just found my parents' divorce papers, and reading the whole story devastated me. I saw my father in a different light. The handsome, commanding, adoring daddy whom I had longed for was small, petty and mean. My mother, it seemed, had hidden so many things from me — important things, which I felt I deserved to know.

I cried on Yeslam's shoulder. I told him that I could never get married because I never wanted my children to be abandoned by their father, as my father had done. I never wanted them to suffer through a bitter divorce, like my parents'. Yeslam gave me comfort and I felt safe with him.

Yeslam had an elegant way about him. One

night he tried to teach me to drive in his Porsche, which I smashed into my mother's gateway. I thought he'd be upset, but he didn't seem to really mind. He just smiled and said, 'You're a dangerous driver.' Yeslam liked his brand new car, but that night I realized he liked me even more. Driving was one of Yeslam's passions, and he had taken lessons in racing-car driving in Sweden. We spent afternoons together speeding across the Swiss mountains, Schubert blaring on the car stereo.

At the beginning of our love affair I saw Yeslam only as a boyfriend, not as a prospective suitor. One of the things that most attracted me to him was that he seemed so independent, and I wanted so much to be independent too. I loved to talk with him, but when he sulked it drove me crazy. He never told me off, but if I spent too much time talking with my friends he would go quiet, and instantly I felt guilty. He wanted all my attention, all the time. He was so reserved with everyone except me. He loved that I was outgoing, but I didn't want to make him uncomfortable — I understood that there were limits. Strangely, his possessiveness flattered me. It felt reassuring.

Our affair was becoming more than just a summer romance. Yeslam began involving me in his private life, introducing me to his extended family. He told me that he had twenty-four brothers and twenty-nine sisters. I couldn't even begin to imagine what that really meant in practical terms, and I suppose my shock showed on my face, because Yeslam assured me this was an unusually large family, even by Saudi Arabian standards.

I met Yeslam's eldest brother, Salem, when he passed through Switzerland. I was impressed by how open and gregarious he was compared to Yeslam. Salem had a great sense of fun, he laughed a lot and played 'Oh, Susannah' on the harmonica. He seemed very westernized, unlike Yeslam. But I could also see there was a complex power struggle underlying their relationship. Though he can't have been more than thirty years old, Salem had an almost paternal attitude towards Yeslam, and Yeslam resented it.

'Salem thinks that just because he's the head of the family, he's in charge of me,' he said, with barely restrained annoyance. 'But I don't need Salem's permission to do anything.' It seemed we shared a struggle — me with my mother; Yeslam with his brother.

One afternoon, as the summer ended, we were walking with Yeslam's dogs in my mother's garden and began talking about the future. Yeslam said he wanted to return to Saudi Arabia and breed Dobermanns. I thought that was ludicrous because I saw great potential in Yeslam. I felt he was exceptional. I told him he was too intelligent to be content with that, and that he owed it to himself to have more ambition. He had to keep studying and make something of his life. Yeslam said, 'I will, but only if you marry me.' It was like a challenge, a kind of dare, and in a way, I heard it as an appeal. Yeslam, too, was waiting for someone to show him his path, so I knew it wasn't a joke. I laughed and said I'd think about it. But we both knew that I meant yes.

Yeslam stayed on at my mother's house after the summer ended. He was my fiancé now, which meant I was a grown-up, which meant I was free. There was a man in the family, as there hadn't been for many years, and my mother loved that. In a way I think she felt that her rebellious daughter was someone else's responsibility now. She no longer questioned me about where I was going when I went out, or demanded I return at fixed hours.

We went out to nightclubs like any other young couple. Yeslam was a good dancer, but not as exuberant as Salem. Yeslam told me pointedly that I shouldn't dance with Salem if he asked me to. If I did, then Salem might get the wrong impression of me. This was one of my first introductions to the many odd rules of his culture. If you dance with another man — even your boyfriend's brother — you're not respected.

Our first disagreement took place in the train station at Lausanne. I wanted something to eat, and there was a long line of people waiting to buy sandwiches. Yeslam went straight up to the sandwich vendor, but the man rather rudely ordered him to take his place in the line. Yeslam did something unexpected: he threw down a hundred Swiss franc note on the counter and walked off. That Yeslam had marched to the front of the queue was one thing, perhaps he hadn't understood that the other people were waiting to be served, but to throw down a large amount of money and walk off? It was so strange.

Later, I told him I didn't understand his reaction, that to me it seemed as though he had rewarded the man for his rudeness. But Yeslam couldn't tolerate being told what to do by a stranger. He didn't submit and go back to queue up, he didn't rage at the man either. He threw money at him to show his scorn. To Yeslam, this was logical. For the first time, though, I found his behaviour puzzling.

29

Yeslam and I became formally engaged in October. My mother now felt certain that I would marry Yeslam — that gave her peace of mind and brought me freedom. In November, Yeslam took me to Lebanon, the birthplace of one of my favourite philosophers, Khalil Gibran, whose book, *The Prophet*, had been my constant companion as a teenager. It was a glorious place, like a fairy tale. I was a grown-up woman travelling with a man who loved me. To me, Lebanon was part of the Arab world, a civilization which had been the home of visionary and wise men who had discovered the secrets of the stars and mathematics. Beirut before the civil war was like the Arabia of the *Thousand and One Nights*: the opulence, the colours, the smells, and above all, the orange-yellow sunlight of the Mediterranean. Yeslam was endlessly attentive. We stayed up late and ate what we liked, did as we wanted to. It was wonderful to be in love. It gave me a new perspective on my life.

It seemed like everywhere we went we encountered more of Yeslam's brothers. In Lebanon we met Ali and Tabet. Physically they were very different. Ali was tall, very Middle Eastern and his mother was Lebanese. Tabet was black and his mother was Ethiopian. It was only then that I realized that

30

Yeslam's father had had twenty-two wives. Rather than let the implications sink in, I chose to see it as an exotic backdrop. I was in love and this labyrinth of family ties was all just another hazy part of my wonderful romance.

We went on to Iran, where we spent three days with some of my mother's relatives, though not my grandmother who was having treatment in America. There, the scales fell from my eyes. As a child, on vacations, I had seen beggars in the street as they came often to my grandmother's neighbourhood for handouts of food or old clothes. One of my uncles would always dismiss our pity, saying 'Oh, don't fret so. They have money, they just don't want to work.'

When Yeslam took me to the carpet bazaar in Tehran to buy a Persian carpet, I saw terrible misery. Small boys and old men were doubled over under bales of carpets. They should have been in school, or at home. They seemed far too fragile to be working. Instead they were laden like donkeys. My life had been so sheltered. I had never seen such a thing and I started crying.

Yeslam took me back to the car. Our driver tried to console me. He said 'You think those people are poor? They're lucky — they have work. I can take you to where families live in holes dug out of the earth.' It made it worse: I was inconsolable. Even Yeslam couldn't comfort me. I realized that the Iran I recalled from childhood had been an illusion, based on a harsh reality that I had never even seen. Everything that had seemed certain was based on secrets and mirages. Later, when I imagined that Saudi Arabia would resemble my childhood memories of Iran, I would be fooling myself twice over.

I was still hesitating about marrying Yeslam. I was young and the bitter example of my parents was still very vivid for me. Marriage was scary, but we had told my mother of our plans. The machine had begun rolling and it was carrying me with it.

In December 1973 we flew to America, to register for university. America was thrilling. It was my childhood dream come true. People really did live lives that were carefree and easygoing. They seemed so much less tied down by convention than anyone I had ever known. I loved the huge spaces, the way of life; the sense of freedom and the incredible sense of stepping into the future.

America truly seemed to be the land of opportunity, and not just for studying. It was clear to Yeslam and to me that this incredibly open country offered us business opportunities too. On our first visit to look at the campus of the University of Southern California, in Los Angeles, we met Jerry Vulk, the director of international students. (He told us later he'd spotted us as foreigners right away. My skirt and high heels, and Yeslam's European suit, made us stand out a mile.) Jerry took us under his wing, and showed us around. We decided to start classes right away, in the month of January. Yeslam would be studying business. I would have to take remedial English.

Then we flew back to Geneva for our first Christmas together, with my family. Yeslam seemed perfectly happy. He didn't seem at all shocked that although my mother was Iranian and a Muslim, we had a Christmas tree and exchanged presents — that we celebrated what is, after all, a very Christian holiday.

A couple of weeks after our first semester began, we met Jerry's wife, Mary Martha Barkley. It was her birthday, and later on, she always called us her birthday gift. Sometimes in life you meet someone you connect with immediately; for me, Mary Martha was like that. She was a real lady, tall, with dark hair and blue eyes — a great beauty. The more I saw of Mary Martha, the more I liked her. She had a wonderful way of carrying herself, a sense of style, and great warmth. She was kind and helped Yeslam and me find a house to rent — the first in a long series of thoughtful and gracious gestures. In short, she adopted us.

Mary Martha became my role model, my ideal American. Her example helped me resolve the loose ends of my personality, helped me to become the adult I aspired to be. Watching Mary Martha, I felt bits of the puzzle of my upbringing falling into place. I loved her nature: independent but tender, optimistic and funny, elegant and direct in her speech. I admired the way she related to her teenaged children and taught them to grow strong and true. Mary Martha was an utterly devoted mother. She woke at four every morning to take her son to swimming practice, and yet she never seemed to pressure her children to act against their will.

I thought, this was the way I would bring up my own children: to be themselves. Mary Martha never judged me, or sought to direct my life as my mother did. We became more than friends; we developed a deep and enduring bond. I admired her more than anyone in the world, and she never disappointed me. She was like a mother to me, and over the years became my American mom.

One of the students in my English class was a Saudi named Abdelatif. He was dumbstruck when he heard I was engaged to Yeslam Bin Ladin. He came up to me one day, very formally, to say that he had known Yeslam's father, who had died in 1967. On the other side of the world, Abdelatif was the first person to open my eyes to the body of Saudi legends surrounding Sheikh Mohamed Bin Laden. He said his own father had worked for Sheikh Mohamed in Jeddah, indeed, almost everyone in Jeddah did. Yeslam's father had been born with nothing, and had built one of the most powerful construction companies in the Middle East, Abdelatif told me. Sheikh Mohamed had built the palaces of kings and princes, and renovated the holiest sites of Islam. He was a giant among men; a hero who worked harder than anyone on earth. He was honest, pious and beloved by everyone who met him. And I was in love with his son.

We invited Abdelatif and his wife for dinner. Later, she taught me to cook Saudi food. (I still make those recipes — sambousas, minced meat in pastry, remain one of my children's favourites.) But then, I was an inexperienced cook, so we also ate a lot of takeout that year. Abdelatif's wife was young, but she dressed modestly, like an old lady, in drab long skirts. A headscarf was always tightly clamped around her face. She was very reserved. Abdelatif was always rather shy with me, too, especially in class, when Yeslam wasn't around. He never seemed to look me in the eyes. I thought then that it was because of the Bin Laden connection. It was only much later that I realized he was not permitted to look at the face of a woman who belonged to another Saudi man.

But Saudi Arabia was far away in those carefree days. Yeslam had left the country as a young boy — he was just six when Sheikh Mohamed sent him to boarding school in Lebanon, and later to England and Sweden, and he had spent only summers at home after that. I had no plans to live in faraway Saudi Arabia. And we were so happy in America. I felt that Yeslam was building our future in this wonderful, free new country that we were discovering. America was our home now.

And if one day Yeslam's destiny took him to Saudi Arabia, so be it. His father had taken the kingdom of Saudi Arabia from sandy camel paths to high-rises and airports. Yeslam, with my help, could encourage it to grow further, to become a modern society. In those days, I had no fear and felt no limits. I had found my life's partner and I felt I could take on the world. My temerity knew no bounds. I knew nothing.

4

My Saudi Wedding

I had a little stone that I'd picked up from my great-aunt's grave in Iran. It lay on my dressing table, set in a bit of silver on a chain. It was just a piece of gravel really, but I treasured it. The day I'd picked it up, standing by that grave with Yeslam, I'd felt in need of guidance. It was as if I asked my great-aunt a question: should I marry this man? The stone had come to stand as a kind of symbol of my relationship with Yeslam. Now, I realized one April morning in our Los Angeles house, I couldn't find my little stone.

'That's it!' I announced to Yeslam. 'It means we can't get married.'

Yeslam took it very seriously. He could be so disarming. He hunted everywhere, he even emptied the garbage, and then triumphantly discovered my precious stone in the back of my dresser. 'Now you have to marry me,' he crowed. That's when I realized how much I meant to Yeslam. He really did deeply want me to marry him.

My mother kept pressuring us to give her a date for our wedding. She liked Yeslam, I think she felt confident that he could temper my impetuous character. And she was so eager to have a man in the family again. So Yeslam and I finally decided that when term ended, I would return to Geneva while Yeslam went to Saudi Arabia to make arrangements for us to be married before the summer ended. Saudis may marry foreigners only if the King gives his authorization, and Yeslam needed to go there to get his permission.

I wanted us to get married in Geneva, among all my family and friends. After all, the Bin Ladens had the means to make such a trip. But when Yeslam returned with the King's permission, he told me he wanted us to marry in Jeddah, his family home. He said that would prove to all that the King had officially agreed that Yeslam could marry me, a foreigner. Yeslam said that people might not respect me as much if we married abroad. Again, there was the peculiar need to earn respect, and the strange, almost feudal rituals with which I would have to earn it. It amazed me that the King's official permission would make me more worthy of respect. It seemed funny, not threatening.

Preparations were already under way for

the wedding of one of his sisters, Regaih. Yeslam told me it would be easiest if ours was scheduled for the same day — 8 August 1974. I couldn't begin to imagine what a Saudi wedding would be like. I had never even been there. I didn't question it. I was in love; my mother was delighted that I was getting married. For me this wedding was increasingly becoming just a formality. I brought no friends: getting visas for me and my family was ordeal enough. There was only my mother, my sisters, and Mamal, the son of my great-aunt, who came from Iran.

I chose not to ask my father to come — I didn't want my mother to have to confront him after all these years. I felt that my mother still loved him, and that seeing him would cause her too much pain. So Mamal was my closest male relative, although I didn't know him well. Mamal would participate in the men-only religious ceremony, where he would represent the bride, and take Yeslam's hand. His presence would certify that Yeslam and I could be married. Without Mamal, it seemed, there could be no wedding. It felt as though his presence was almost as important as my own.

It seemed like such a droll concept. Whenever she caught sight of Mamal, my sister Magnolia used to joke, 'Look, here comes the bride!'

My preparations were hurried. First I went out to buy a wedding dress. I looked at the haute couture at Chanel in Geneva, but none of the models were anything like the dress I wanted, or what I thought suitable for Saudi Arabia, based on my childhood memories of Iran. I wanted a high collar, scalloped sleeves with a cuff, something completely simple and yet perfectly elegant. In the end I designed a dress that was made up by a Chanel tailor, in white organza. I felt it was truly me.

Next came the veils. A long wedding veil in white organza too, and the black cloak that would shield my face and body from the world around me in Yeslam's country. Yeslam had explained that I would need one. I bought the thick black cotton and had it made up. The result was a heavy Persian veil, like a chador, not the thinner, silk Saudi *abaya*. I didn't know any better. The thing was like a curtain, covering me from head to toe, so heavy it almost stood up on its own. It seemed almost comically antiquated, like wearing a disguise.

Last, my sisters and I went out shopping for the many long dresses which Yeslam had told me we would need. But in all of Geneva we could find nothing even remotely appropriate: dresses that were formal, yet modest, for parties; simpler, day dresses that were not too casual, yet long. We had to have a tailor make up a whole series of garments. Finally, my sisters had salmon-pink bridesmaids' dresses made up too. We were all caught up in a flurry of fittings.

Then Yeslam and I took the plane to Jeddah, with my sister Salomé. My mother and my other two sisters followed us two days later. Yeslam wore the white cotton Saudi robe called a *tobe*. It is quite crisp and elegant when it is done well: I thought him even more romantic in this exotic costume. A few minutes before we landed, Salomé and I put on our veils. We were covered completely in thick black cloth — hands, head, body. Just our feet stuck out. Even our eyes were hidden behind the impenetrable black gauze. I looked over at Salomé. It was a shock. She had no face.

I watched the desert approach as we landed. The light through the black gauze cloth was so dim, I didn't know if this new country was simply the darkest, emptiest place I had ever seen, or if the cloth across my eyes was preventing me from seeing anything that was there. It gave me a strange, oppressive feeling. This was not like when I had tried the veil on at the tailor's in Geneva.

41

Then I had been excited. I was getting married. But now I felt a sense of melancholy inside me, an apprehension that met the blackness of the outside world.

The heat was stifling. I could hardly breathe under the thick folds of my *abaya*. Every movement was slow and awkward. As we came down the steps of the plane, my sister stumbled. Everything spilled out of her beauty case, and yet nobody helped her up or picked up anything. She turned to me, a completely black speaking triangle, and said 'What is this place?' In Saudi Arabia, no man could touch her, or even come too close.

I was so fixated on keeping the veil in place, I couldn't pay attention to anything else. I caught sight of Yeslam's brother Ibrahim, with his crinkly eyes and friendly face. I called loudly, 'Hi, Ibrahim.' I felt so relieved, to see someone familiar, but he said nothing. He looked almost embarrassed. Then, very softly, he said 'Hi.' Although Yeslam had warned me, I had forgotten that I was not permitted to speak to any man in public.

Just a few minutes in Saudi Arabia and I had already made my first blunder. It was beginning to dawn on me that in Yeslam's country I was going to have to keep quiet in public. We drove off, not even waiting for our suitcases. Some nameless underling would take care of that now. I looked out of the car window and through my veil I saw just a dim light — no people, no buildings. Even the street-lights were dark.

In fact, there was very little to see. Jeddah, at the time, was just a small town, dingy and old, and the neighbourhood where most of the Bin Ladens lived together was on the road out towards Mecca, at the very edge of the desert. The road went bumpy, then smooth, and suddenly we were at Yeslam's home — Kilometre Seven on the Mecca Road. The gate was open and my mother-in-law was standing on the threshold of the house.

We always called my mother-in-law Om Yeslam. She had a name of her own, of course, but it was never used. Like most women in the Kingdom, she took the name of her eldest son. If she has only daughters, a Saudi woman carries the name of her first-born until a son comes, and then his name supersedes his sister's.

Om Yeslam was pleasant and welcoming. It was a relief to be able to take off my *abaya*. Suddenly the light inside the house seemed blinding. There were so many chandeliers lit up, it was like stepping into a lamp shop. We sat down and made small talk. After the first greetings, I began to take in my new surroundings. Everything inside the house seemed to be green. Dark green wall-to-wall carpeting, green wallpaper, green-gold velvet sofas arranged around the four walls of the sitting room. There were no rich old carpets or fine antique workmanship. The house was new and awkward, like a raw suburban tract home. It was really quite odd-looking. There were plastic flowers, too. When I went to wash, I discovered my bedroom had a dark maroon marble bathroom with no windows. It was like a tomb.

The servants came in with the evening meal. They spread a cloth on the floor and we ate there: *lebna* cheese, honey, cucumber salad, flat bread, yogurt and bean paste. The lack of sophistication surprised me. I had imagined an exotic Oriental abode, like in the movies or my grandmother's home in Iran. After all, Yeslam's father had been one of the richest men in Saudi Arabia. But this was just a basic house where people lived very simply. It was not at all the life of refinement and elegance I had imagined.

My mother-in-law was a soft-spoken and amiable woman. She was never harsh with me, although I know she must have been disappointed that her son had not chosen to marry a Saudi girl. We chatted. Our conversation was stilted, in Farsi and English, interspersed with Yeslam's translations into Arabic.

The next day the round of visitors commenced. Since I was a bride-to-be, the family had to come to congratulate me — and, more importantly, to examine me. I faced an endless stream of women — only women — all in formal, long dresses, laden down with lots of jewellery. There were dozens of them. They had unfamiliar names that I found difficult to retain. It was a blur. Most of the visitors were Yeslam's relatives. The abstract idea of twenty-two wives, twenty-five sons and twenty-nine daughters was beginning to take form before my eyes. It was bewildering.

Salem, whom I had already met in Geneva, was then about thirty; he was the eldest son. Yeslam was the tenth in line. Nobody told me the order of birth of the sisters as they flowed through the door. It manifestly didn't matter, and I didn't even think to ask.

Of course Yeslam's father, Sheikh Mohamed, hadn't been married to all his wives at the same time. He divorced some as he married others. Most of the wives, divorced or current, as well as their children, had lived inside the patriarch's huge compound in Jeddah while Yeslam was growing up. But just before Sheikh Mohamed died, he had begun building a number

45

of new houses, seven kilometres along the Mecca Road out of town. Many of his children moved there after his death, and took their mothers along with them. It was a whole Bin Laden neighbourhood of separate houses, laid out along three streets that were isolated at the edge of the desert.

We lived those first days in Kilometre Seven in almost hypnotic inactivity. There was nothing to do except welcome an endless rustling of female visitors in formal clothes and drink cardamom-spiced Arabic coffee in tiny cups. At first, I didn't know I should shake my cup to signify that I had had enough, and didn't want to be served any more. I've never drunk so much coffee in my life! Finally, when I explained my problem, Om Yeslam kindly explained.

Only the men could come and go as they pleased. We women were confined to the house — not only because of the sweltering summer heat, but because we should not be seen unveiled by men outside the family. Even to go into the garden we had to notify the male employees to vacate the premises. Once the coast was clear, we would step out, usually at dusk, into a furnace. The desert sand around us was blinding, it was like staring at Alpine snow without sunglasses. In this way, my free-wheeling universe had

46

shrunk to one and a half acres of baking garden, planted with a few spindly trees.

We took no exercise. Walking anywhere was completely unthinkable. There was, in any case, nowhere we could go. Hotels, sports arenas, theatres, swimming pools, restaurants, if they existed at all, were only for men. Even ice-cream parlours, parks and shops were forbidden: a woman of respect could almost never shop. No male other than Yeslam could see my face. True, Yeslam had warned me about all this before I'd arrived. But living it was very different. It was unreal.

Om Yeslam's life was entirely sealed off from any men, apart from her relatives. Her Ethiopian driver never saw her unveiled. I'm not sure if he ever even heard her voice. Her young houseboy, who was about twelve and also Ethiopian, would take her orders and instruct the driver when to be ready and where to go.

I remember the look of astonishment and dismay that passed between my mother-in-law and Yeslam's sister, Fawzia, when I first thanked their maid, just for something trivial, like a cup of tea. It was quite startling. And I remember the surprise, and a kind of joy, that sprang into that young woman's face. My mother's family had plenty of servants in Iran, as a matter of course, and even in

47

Switzerland we had a governess. But this was another world, and there was something unpleasant about it.

Later I was to visit many houses, and surprise many women by thanking their servants. This contempt for the staff highlighted the fact that Saudi Arabia was one of the last countries in the world to outlaw slavery. Until 1962 it was still common for grand families to own slaves. The government finally bought their freedom. Fifteen years later, servants were still largely not considered to be autonomous human beings worthy of thanks.

Every gesture in this strange new world seemed foreign. The people around me were inscrutable. Men could not look at me, even veiled. The family was friendly, but I could not read anything in their eyes. It was almost ethereal, this monotonous denial. I felt hypnotized. It was nothing like Iran or Beirut — it was a completely different world. There were so many things to absorb at once, and I didn't know what to think of them.

I discovered the city of Jeddah in daylight when we went to the Swiss embassy to register our imminent marriage, after three days in the country. If I did not record that I wished to retain my nationality prior to the wedding I would lose my Swiss passport.

Later, I was to bless that day many times. It was my first release from the house. The air was so hot I could hardly breathe under the thick veil. Yeslam had to remind me that I must sit in the back of the car, completely covered, while he drove.

Driving through Jeddah, staring from behind the tinted windows of the Mercedes, I watched a roadside scene from another millennium. In those days Saudi Arabia was still emerging from the crushing poverty of its traditional way of life. People were less poor after oil was discovered in the 1930s, but the crazy bonanza of wealth that would sweep over the country after the 1973 oil embargo lay in the future. Donkey Square was a criss-cross of dirt tracks where people came to buy water from men leading donkeys with barrels on their backs. Shimmering waves of heat rose off the city's few tarmac roads. I saw one or two squalid little shops. Scattered across the endless sand dunes were the houses, invisible behind the tall concrete walls that protected their women from view.

At first I wasn't even aware of what seemed so strange about this country, but then it hit me: half the population of Saudi Arabia is kept behind walls, all the time. It was hard to fathom a city with almost no women. I felt like a ghost: women didn't exist in this world of men. This place that was arid and almost colourless. Apart from the sand, which covered the roads with a soft, dusty carpet, the only colours that stood out were black and white. The men's white *tobes*, and a very few stark black triangles of cloth: the shrouded women. Geneva was a thousand years away.

A few days later, Yeslam planned an outing for us to the Red Sea, to alleviate our sense of confinement. But the whole experience only emphasized how strange Saudi Arabia really was. My sisters and I had neglected to pack swimsuits. So, in our Western ways, we girls debated how and when we should go shopping.

But as a woman could not shop in public, the driver was summoned and instructed by the houseboy to go and buy some swimsuits. When he returned, the houseboy presented us with two suitcases full of various, properly modest one-piece suits. This, for many Saudi women at the time, was shopping. Numbed with the strangeness of it all, we selected items we would never ordinarily have dreamt of ever wearing.

We were ready for the beach. I would be meeting some of Yeslam's older brothers for the first time: Omar, a devout, conservative man; Bakr, stern and dour; and Mahrouz, who was becoming increasingly religious, despite being very Westernized — and, in fact, something of a playboy.

The Bin Ladens owned six or seven bungalows by the ocean, rickety little one-room cabins, really, with kitchenettes and a shared generator. The compound was fenced by cement blocks that stretched right into the sea. The brothers solemnly retired to one cabin, and my sisters and I went out to the sea. We lowered ourselves into the water by a rusty ladder off the wooden jetty, and we swam. Om Yeslam watched us, smiling, but ready to warn away any careless men. I'd heard the Red Sea was a scuba-diver's paradise; the scenery was beautiful, and it certainly was the bluest sea I'd ever seen. We dressed again, and drank tea and warm Coke. There were flies everywhere. An effort had been made to amuse us, so we acted amused.

But then Yeslam asked me not to smoke in front of his brothers. It was a trivial request, but after the tension of those first days in Jeddah, I was suddenly overcome with frustration. It seemed that I was to have no say now even in the smallest acts of my daily life. Would I have to deny every aspect of my personality in the struggle to fit into this deeply foreign, tightly constraining country? I snapped, 'I will not smoke, but I will not marry you either.' I meant it — it was the end.

True to his Saudi upbringing, Yeslam avoided an argument. But later, when we were seated together drinking tea, he casually offered me a cigarette in front of his family. That surprising gesture of support gave me hope and dispelled some of my apprehension about the future. It was a small concession, but I felt it was a symbol. With Yeslam's help and understanding, I would manage to remain myself in this bewildering society.

We made another special excursion, only my third sortie from the house in ten days. Om Yeslam and Fawzia took us to the gold souk. It seemed to be one of the only public places a Bin Laden woman ever went to. Walking around in a crowd of faceless, black-shrouded women was an oddly difficult feat. As I looked around me, I realized I couldn't recognize the family — not even my own sisters — amid all the other black triangles. When I dawdled, I had to call out to Fawzia to come and get me.

Gold gleamed everywhere in the souk, bright enough to see even through the dim veil. The shop we went into was tiny, hung from ceiling to floor with gold bracelets and chains and thick rings. These weren't priced by workmanship, but by weight, and then the price totted up on an abacus. While we were still making our selection, the call rang out for prayer, and the salesmen rushed outside, leaving us alone in their shop. We were not permitted to pray in a public space — with the exception of the ritual prayer that is required in the holy cities of Mecca and Medina. We were forbidden even to step into a mosque. But the male shopkeepers had to pray together when the muezzin called. So there we were alone in a room filled with gold and the door wasn't even locked. But in Saudi Arabia there is hardly any theft. The draconian punishment is a mighty deterrent: thieves' hands are simply cut off.

The day I got married was the most bizarre moment of those first, strange few weeks. Yeslam and Ibrahim drove me to the parking lot of an administrative building to register our wedding. I waited, in my *abaya*, in the car, while they went inside. Yeslam and Ibrahim brought out a book for me to sign. It was the marriage register. I was so proud that I had learned to write my name in Arabic letters. Then someone took the book back, and we were married.

I had missed the customary *melka* engagement party, where Regaih had signed her wedding papers amid a ceremonial party of women, weeks before. So I got married, in my black *abaya*, in a sandy parking lot. From the King's permission to a parked car: my wedding had turned out to be so different from what any bride would imagine that it was almost funny. It was as if I was watching someone else get married. I tried to tell myself it didn't really matter.

The double wedding celebration came two days later. We drove to Salem's house, across the road, to get ready. (Many years later I began walking across the road to that house — completely veiled, of course. Such a bold move was the subject of much shocked comment among my female relatives.) There were women everywhere, attended to by armies of hairdressers. I hadn't slept and I had a crushing headache. One of my sisters told me that the women had handed around my dress in my absence, and had clucked over it before they brought it to me. I suppose they thought it was too simple. I felt scorned, and upset — it seemed so inconsiderate.

I dressed, and my hair was done up in an old-fashioned chignon. I was tense with nerves. Over my white organza dress went that baleful, stiff black chador. We stepped out to the car in the evening heat and drove to the Candara hotel. I think it was the only hotel in Jeddah at the time. There, in the garden — strung with naked light bulbs as ersatz fairy lights — a separate women's area had been prepared, with jute screens to shield us from the gaze of any passing waiters or male guests.

My eyes met a vast crowd of women. The men's ceremony was taking place elsewhere. Perhaps six hundred guests were massed together, all decked out with jewellery and flounces, as for a grand ceremonial ball. Customarily, a wedding is the only occasion at which women do not veil their faces despite the presence of an unfamiliar man — the groom. Still, though their dresses were by Western designers, most of the women not in Yeslam's immediate family covered their hair with a light headscarf. A few even wore the full *abaya*. They greeted us with a hullabaloo of ululating calls. Their eyes scrutinized me as Yeslam and I approached the canopy.

We were seated, with Regaih and her groom, on a raised dais. Each female guest approached us to be greeted. Only women served at the buffet. A women-only orchestra from Kuwait began the monotonous drumming and atonal Arabic music that I learned, over the years, to appreciate. The women danced the old Bedouin dances in their formal, Western dresses. It is like belly-dancing from Egypt, but jerkier, without the sensual overtones. We sat, under the canopy, on our throne, watching them. They looked askance at my sisters in their salmon pink dresses: it was only then that I realized there are no bridesmaids at a Saudi wedding. My headache drummed at me.

Everyone smiled. At no time in my years in Saudi Arabia did I ever feel any direct hostility. A properly brought-up Saudi is never openly rude — except to a servant. Still, I always knew that I was under intense scrutiny. I and my way of life were as strange to them as they were to me. I was a foreigner. I had been brought up in the West, with my face displayed to all. They had been born in the land of Islam's holiest sites — the homeland of the Prophet Muhammad. They believed they were the chosen guardians of the world's most sacred places. They were the chosen people of God.

As I watched them watching me, all the new and strange and sometimes unpleasant experiences of those first days struck me with full force. I was married now, to a man from a country that I now realized was very different from my own. Perhaps every bride asks herself if she has made the right decision; I wondered if I should not have asked myself

56

this earlier. Sitting up there, with only women at my feet, I felt overwhelmed by a sense of the enormous gap between two civilizations: the world I came from, and the one that I had just entered. The only thing that eased my restlessness and my feeling of being confined, was the knowledge that I would soon return to the blessed normality of America where, on the same night, President Nixon resigned.

5

America

That first, surreal three-week visit should have warned me of all the difficulties that lay ahead of me. It foreshadowed the coming decades, and would forever change the course of my life. But I was young then, and heedless. When we left Saudi Arabia for California, a few days after our wedding party, I felt as if I had escaped. The dull haze in my brain was soon dispelled. I scrunched up my *abaya* and tossed it somewhere, and it was as if nothing had happened: our new American independence engulfed us again.

We attended classes, shopped for our new home, ate in restaurants and went to movies. We spent time with Mary Martha and her family and socialized with other American friends, which was great for Yeslam's burgeoning business. He had managed to fix his schedule so that he attended classes only two days a week, and spent much of the rest of his time exploring opportunities in the new world of personal computers. I took advantage of everything the American way of life could offer me. I was a married woman now, and in charge of my own destiny: I could do as I pleased, I thought blithely.

I learned to drive in Yeslam's white sports car, and he bought me a Pontiac Firebird. Like Yeslam, I loved to drive — loved simply driving about, when I felt restless. Then he bought a little Mooney single-engine plane and persuaded me to take flying lessons. We flew to Santa Barbara together at weekends and to Las Vegas.

One time Yeslam won big at the casino and he bought me a white mink stole — not that he was really a gambler, but sometimes he enjoyed fooling around. He also bought me jewellery. I loved the attention and the romance of it all as much as the presents themselves.

I think Yeslam was happy then. Happier, certainly, than he'd been in his lonely childhood at boarding schools, far from home, and perhaps happier than he ever was again. We read books together and stayed up late at night talking about his studies, his first steps in business, listening to the classical music that he loved, as loud as we liked. Yeslam had bought one of the first personal computers. He sensed a vast potential for investment and business opportunities in that field. He had been to visit a man called Steve Jobs, who was doing something bold and new with computers in his garage. It was all so exciting to us. We shared everything in this brand new America that we were free, now, to discover. We were giddy with the open-endedness of it all.

Ibrahim came to live with us, and attended classes at USC, though he was so lackadaisical about studying that I'm not certain he ever graduated. It made Yeslam, so clever and serious, even more attractive to me. Some of Yeslam's other brothers began visiting us too, on trips abroad, and we would take them to Disneyland, to Las Vegas and to parties. I wore jeans and sneakers; they wore tight trousers and unbuttoned shirts and had Afro hair. They looked just like Americans — on the outside.

Occasionally, Saudi Arabia would come into focus again. Mafouz, Yeslam's milk brother, came to visit us. His mother, Aïsha, was Sheikh Mohamed's eldest child, and she had given birth to Mafouz just as Yeslam's mother was having her first son. Aïsha and Om Yeslam breastfed each other's children. It is a custom in Saudi Arabia, though it must never be done if the children are boy and girl, because it would mean they can never marry.

To be a milk brother creates a special tie.

Mafouz was deeply devout. In Saudi Arabia he wore his *tobe* short, to display his simplicity — that was the sign of the religious man in those days. This was his first trip abroad. Yeslam took him up in his little aeroplane for a joyride, with my sister Salomé. Mafouz spent the whole trip scrunched up in a corner. The seats were close together, and he felt self-conscious and physically repelled, sitting next to a woman who wasn't his relative. His dismay was twofold when Salomé announced that she wasn't feeling well. Poor Mafouz.

In November I realized I was pregnant — the traditional way: I sent Yeslam out again and again for tacos one Sunday morning, and ate myself sick. (Later, I could never bring myself to eat another taco.) I felt surprised that I was really grown-up enough to be expecting a baby, and I was nauseous all the time. Yeslam was glad, of course, and he smiled when I told him, pulling at his little goatee. But he didn't seem as delighted as I'd expected. He was not overwhelmed with joy. He never cuddled my tummy or volunteered his amazement when the baby kicked.

We wanted a son — we both knew that. In a household of women, my sisters and I had always been restricted as children. I had often

61

wished I had a brother. I always felt that a brother would have more freedom, and influence my mother to be less strict. And, of course, Yeslam wanted a boy because he was Saudi: it was as simple as that. Perhaps because of my Iranian background, I understood this without it having to be said.

I had to quit school on doctor's orders, and rest for much of my pregnancy. An American friend of mine, Billy, came to visit. We'd met in Geneva and had always been close. I looked forward to his visit after days of sitting around the house. My swollen belly was so new: what other topic of conversation could there be? I told Billy we hoped for a boy, but Billy said, 'I hope it's a girl. And I hope she'll be just like you. That would be great.' I looked up at Yeslam, smiling. But his face had gone dark. He stared at Billy, not frowning, but he was very still and quiet. Billy left rather quickly. He visited again, but Yeslam managed wordlessly to communicate that Billy was no longer welcome.

In the beginning, you don't see that you're becoming someone else's object. You meet someone and the two of you become one, melding your tastes and personalities until you feel you are invincible. You begin to mute your disagreements, until slowly your own personality becomes submerged in your desire to please. You lose yourself inside the other — the more so, if you are from two different cultures, as Yeslam and I were. Pregnancy made me vulnerable, too; and also youth. It happened so gradually that I couldn't even feel it, but my own personality had begun giving way to Yeslam's.

Mary Martha was a lifeline in those long months of pregnancy. I felt sick all the time and for months I couldn't even step into a car. Mary Martha helped Yeslam hunt for a new, larger house, in Pacific Palisades. She drove me around to buy baby clothes and a crib. She took me to my Lamaze preparation classes, and let me prattle on about the little boy I dreamed of.

One time, Mary Martha was organizing a big charity lunch and could find no helpers, so I rounded up the Bin Ladens. Ibrahim, with his huge, shaggy Afro, waited tables; Yeslam took the money at the door. I, in my expensive silk pregnancy dress, washed the dishes. As she was leaving, one conservative Californian matron took Mary Martha aside. 'Those certainly are some *different* people you have helping you,' she said in a loud stage whisper. 'Where on earth did you find them?'

'Never mind, you could never afford them,' Mary Martha whispered back. In the kitchen, we were weak with laughter.

When Mary Martha's parents visited from Arizona, we would always go to see them. Her father, Les Barkley, had a big agricultural business cultivating iceberg lettuce. He was a big, strong John Wayne-type figure, and her mother was a gracious, intelligent woman, a firm Republican, with a deep sense of honour. We talked about American politics and the American constitution, and about family. We used to do the *Reader's Digest* vocabulary tests together. For her, this was a distraction; for me, essential training.

There was a huge amount of love between the members of Mary Martha's family, and a sense of mutual respect that was new to me. Growing up in my mother's house, I was used to obeying older people unquestioningly — just because they were older. I gave automatic respect and obedience to age and authority. But in Mary Martha's family there was deep acceptance of all the family members. They were well-mannered, but they were also free to speak as they wished — free to disagree.

Being with the Barkleys was a warm and welcoming experience. In that family, every individual was respected, regardless of age. Even a child's opinion was listened to, and carefully acknowledged. Their politeness was not mechanical; it was thoughtful. This was the point of view I took with me later to Saudi Arabia. I strove to bring up my daughters in this spirit. Every day, I grew more strongly anchored to the values of this new, free American culture.

One March morning in 1975, Yeslam woke me with the news that King Faisal had been assassinated — shot by one of his own nephews. Saudi Arabia was in uproar. It was claimed that the assassin was deranged, but most likely it was a revenge killing, Yeslam said the murderer's brother had been executed ten years previously for participating in an Islamic fundamentalist revolt against the King's decision to authorize television in the Kingdom.

I could feel his sense of panic and urgency. Increasingly, Yeslam felt he needed to return to his country and help with the family business. He began rushing through his studies so he could graduate early.

I, meanwhile, gave birth — the most momentous event in my life, and one that would change me for ever. Mary Martha was with me. (I felt Yeslam would not be able to handle the gory details.) The baby was a girl.

Much later, I learned that Yeslam simply walked out when he heard. He turned on his heel and walked out of the hospital. But at the time I was exhausted. When they installed me in my room, and brought me my new baby, all I knew was that Yeslam was there. I thought that perhaps he was a little disappointed, but I was sure we would adjust.

Now we would have to pick out a name. We'd chosen a boy's name, Faisal, but we had never got around to choosing one for a girl. Yeslam settled on Wafah, meaning the faithful one.

Having a girl came as such a surprise to me; and what a nice surprise she would turn out to be. Wafah was beautiful — really unusually good-looking for a new-born — and when I looked at her I couldn't possibly be disappointed. I was overwhelmed with fascination and love. But Yeslam was petulant at times. It was almost as if he was jealous of the hold that little Wafah had on me. Although he came from a large family he was much less attentive to Wafah than I was. He acted happy when I pointed out the new things she was doing, such as sucking her toes or reaching out for toys, but I did always have to point them out.

Soon after Wafah was born, Mary Martha took me out shopping. I thought it would be good for Yeslam to bond with the baby alone. Wafah still needed to be fed every two hours, so we raced around buying baby clothes. When we came back, Yeslam held her out to me, like a package. 'She's wet,' he said. 'You should change her.' Yeslam was so silly, I mused. Hadn't it occurred to him to change her himself? I felt so tender towards him. His haplessness made me feel even more confident and capable in my new role as a mother.

For me, Wafah was like a miracle. For the first time in my life I was completely responsible for another human being. Like all new mothers, I promised myself I wouldn't make the same mistakes my own mother had. I would respect my baby's character and let her grow free to become whatever person already lay, furled up, inside her perfect little body.

I didn't want to hire a nanny (though we did, at that point, have a maid to cook and clean). It was I who woke up to feed Wafah at night, though Yeslam grumbled. I propped Wafah up beside me and talked to her all day long. She'd look back at me, clear-eyed, as if she'd understood every word. I truly enjoyed walking my baby through the park in her new buggy, playing with her in the sunlight, smelling the wonderful babyness in the folds of her neck. She was a stubborn little thing, with a fiercely strong character. For months after she was weaned she refused to eat anything except ready-made Gerber Turkey and Rice dinners, and even Mary Martha's good home cooking couldn't tempt her.

I flooded our house with music — Cat Stevens, Shirley Bassey, Charles Aznavour, Jacques Brel — twirling my lovely little girl round the living room. She went to sleep accompanied by Tchaikovsky on her own hi-fi system, surrounded by a department-store's worth of toys. Nothing was too good for my Wafah.

I never returned to college, though I lived through every term-paper and exam at Yeslam's side as he raced through the syllabus. His mind was quick and incisive. I admired his intelligence, his discipline and his rapid grasp of complex facts. As his graduation came closer, his plans to take us back to Saudi Arabia became more urgent. After the oil embargo of 1973, when the price of crude oil rose, and money began pouring into Saudi Arabia, Yeslam realized that new opportunities for business were opening up, and he wanted to be a part of it. He told me it would be great for our new family. I knew it meant renouncing my hopes to return to college, that it meant renouncing many things. But, lulled in my cosy joy at life with my beloved little Wafah and my clever, handsome husband, I agreed.

6

Life with the Bin Ladens

We moved to Jeddah in the fall of 1976. This time, as we circled the airport, I had a proper, thin silk Saudi *abaya* but the heavy feeling that I had forgotten returned as I cloaked myself in the impenetrable gauze, and this time it felt stronger. I would not be leaving after two weeks. This was not a veil that I could one day scuff up in a ball and forget at the back of a closet. This *abaya*, now, would accompany me everywhere and symbolize my life.

For years, the first thing people asked me when I travelled abroad was 'Do you wear the veil?' And when I said yes, I always used to get a kick out of how astonished and appalled they were. Of course, in practical terms, the veil was an inconvenience. It was an insult to my intelligence and to my freedom, but I didn't make a big drama out of it. To cover my unease, in those early days, I accepted the Saudi explanation that the *abaya* symbolized respect for women. More fundamentally, I was convinced that it would be temporary.

I am an optimist by nature. Jeddah was booming, and foreigners had begun flocking to the country. The menacing emptiness of the desert all around would, after a short time, give way to vast new roads and shiny skyscrapers. I assumed that Saudi society would move into the modern world, just as other cultures had. Soon, I thought — as in Iran — the veil would be something that women could choose to wear — or not. We would also, as a matter of course, be able to walk around the streets, or drive where we wanted. We would shop on our own: there would soon be shops; we would work, if we wished to.

Meanwhile, I had to adjust to my new life and try to become a good Saudi wife and mother. We moved in with Om Yeslam and Fawzia. I shared Om Yeslam's Sudanese driver, Abdou, and we hired another Ethiopian maid. I gradually picked up basic Arabic, and, as Wafah cut her teeth and toddled about, I found motherhood absorbing. Other than that, nothing about my new life came naturally.

Strangest of all was becoming enfolded into Om Yeslam's quiet, unhurried life, in her woman's world. It was like going under an anaesthetic. Om Yeslam was a good woman, but her only interests were cooking and the Koran. She prayed five times a day, and she lived in a world that was strictly confined within an invisible cage of tradition.

The Arabic word for woman, *hormah*, derives from the word *haram*: sin; and every moment of Om Yeslam's life was intertwined with her observation of the rituals and rules of Islamic custom. Everything seemed to be *haram*, or sinful; and if it wasn't sinful it was *abe*, shameful. It was *haram* to play music, *abe* to walk around in the street; *abe* to talk to a male servant, *haram* to be seen by a man outside the family. Om Yeslam was a tolerant woman, and her still, calm face rarely frowned, but I could infer her disapproval of my behaviour from her always politely voiced surprise.

It was, of course, almost always *haram* and *abe* for a Bin Laden woman to leave the house. Our faces could never be seen by a man outside the family. If we left the house, it was to be driven somewhere specific by a man. It was months before I even understood the layout of the neighbourhood.

Shopping was for servants. If we needed something, Abdou or another driver would have to be instructed by the houseboy to search for the required item. It wasn't just swimsuits. It was tea, or sanitary towels

— anything at all. If we didn't like them, he would return with another suitcase full. We would select something, he would go back to the shop with the suitcase, ascertain the price, and return again for the payment. These rigmaroles drove me insane.

The system that constricted all women in a mesh of restraints made every basic gesture of my life unbelievably complex. Wafah was accustomed to drinking Similac baby milk. Though I'd brought a large stock, it was running out. I felt she lacked energy, though perhaps it was the heat. I was concerned that she might be allergic to other brands so I was determined to find Similac for her. I sent Abdou out for some, but he returned time and again with a barrel of basic baby milk. Finding Similac became obsessively important to me. I couldn't believe that there were only two kinds of baby milk available in the entire country. One night, I told Yeslam he absolutely had to let me go to the grocery store so that I could check myself. He acquiesced.

I would go to the grocery store! What a step forward! I was jubilant. Abdou and Yeslam drove me there, abaya-ed from head to toe. Yeslam asked me to wait in the car and disappeared into the shop. Finally, after ten minutes he guided me to the entrance. I walked past a line of about a dozen men standing outside the door, all stiffly facing away from me. Once I stepped inside, my hopes crumbled. The store was a shabby, windowless prefab, dusty and crowded with cardboard boxes filled with cans. It smelled like a warehouse. Even finding the milk was difficult — everything was in unlabelled boxes. There was hardly any choice, and certainly no Similac. And in order that one completely black-shrouded woman could walk inside with her husband, the store had been emptied of all its clients and staff.

What on earth did they fear — contamination? Could it really be a sign of politeness and respect for these men to turn their backs on me because I was a woman? I was overcome with rage. Just a few weeks before, I had raced through a brightly lit Californian supermarket, grabbing fresh fruit and cereal for my family. I returned home, a bitter knot of hopeless homesickness in the pit of my stomach. I felt I'd entered an alien, parallel universe.

I needed activity. I needed to read. I longed for some stimulation of my mind and my body. The two TV channels broadcast an imam chanting the Koran all day; for lighter fare, little boys as young as six or seven, who had won prizes for their Koranic knowledge, recited the holy texts from memory. Foreign newspapers were magic-markered into fragments: any comment on Saudi Arabia or Israel, any photo or advertisement showing even one inch of a woman's body was blacked out by the censors. I held them up to the light, to divine the forbidden words veiled by the censor's pen.

There were no books, no theatres, no concerts and no cinemas. There was no reason to go out, and in any case we could not go out: I was not allowed to go for a walk, and legally could not drive. Much as I loved my role as a mother, taking care of Wafah was not enough to fill my mind and my days. I had to get out. I told Yeslam I was desperate. He understood and proposed we make a three-day trip to Geneva to buy books, and some Similac, and to assuage my homesickness. As often happened during those first few years in Saudi Arabia, when I forced myself to complain, Yeslam found a way to reassure me. I revived: my husband was on my side.

In Geneva, my familiar world looked startlingly different. I gazed at it all with new eyes. Suddenly everything I had taken for granted all my life seemed marvellous. Just five hours away from the brown, dry, vacant land around the Jeddah airport, here was a complex landscape filled with life. There were so many houses and people, such richly coloured fields and gardens. I found myself staring at the sharp blue-grey mountains, trying to memorize each jagged edge. Even the trees in my mother's garden seemed powerfully significant. I stared at the shapes and colours of the autumn leaves, soaking them into my brain. It was as though I was seeing them for the first time. I bought piles of books and basic supplies. Then I steeled myself for our return.

During our first year in Saudi Arabia, Yeslam travelled often for his first job in his family's corporation. He went mostly to Dammam, a rapidly developing port on the eastern coast which had been built to serve the oil industry. Staying alone in Jeddah for two or three days at a time, with Om Yeslam and Fawzia my only adult companions, drove me half-mad with boredom, with or without my stash of books.

I spent most of my days alone with Om Yeslam. Fawzia attended university and she was studying business, but it was not like any university I knew. Her 'classes' were, in reality, video presentations by male professors who could not be permitted to teach directly in a strictly segregated, women-only class-room. There was a library, but women students had to apply for books in writing, and received them from an office reserved for that purpose a week later. I never saw Fawzia read a book, or heard her talk about her studies.

I could feel myself sinking into lassitude. I felt bored and aimless as a goldfish, swimming slower and slower inside an absolutely smooth glass bowl, with nothing to do, gulping for air.

The heat crushed us all into submission. During the day we never left the air-conditioned house. Stepping out into the garden at dusk was like walking into a furnace. The first time I saw Om Yeslam animated was when it rained. We woke up one morning to a grey sky, and everyone talked excitedly about rain coming. As the first droplets fell, Om Yeslam and Fawzia rushed out into the garden. 'It's raining, it's raining,' they cried. 'Come out and see.' I knew what rain was — this at last was something I knew very well — but to please them I emerged. The wet sand smelled unpleasant, but it didn't matter: it was raining and that made them happy. The garden flooded, with a foot or so of water washing around the concrete walls. For a couple of days the sand grew green, as if even the desert was grateful. Later, I too would dash out into the rain, for joy at some slight change in the routine of my life.

The sandstorms were less pleasant. Sharp shards of sand would be whipped up by a wheeling, cutting wind. The sky would darken, sometimes for days. Clouds of dust entered everywhere, through closed doors and windows, creeping into your clothes, your shoes and food. It was uncomfortable and frightening; the noise was sinister. I never grew accustomed to it. Afterwards the gardener would sweep the sand back into the desert, a futile gesture which always gave me pause. We were living in a place that was never meant for human habitation. Though Jeddah is on the sea — it is a major port — the desert is ever-present, stony and wild, constantly encroaching on life. It has not even one river, no gentle natural greens, no mellow colours.

The desert of Saudi Arabia is beautiful in a way: the wavy sand-dunes, the striking light, and the wide, vast horizon made me think of the ocean. But it is immense and monotonous — utterly empty. A kingdom carved from the desert is a forbidding place. Until the nineteenth century no European had ever even entered the vast, isolated desert that is Saudi Arabia. Physically, it is perhaps the most unwelcoming country on the planet.

7

The Patriach

Socially, Saudi Arabia is medieval, dark with sin and interdiction. The Saudi version of Islam — Wahhabism — is ferocious in its enforcement of an ancient social code. This is not a complex, intellectual culture like that of Iran, or Egypt. The Kingdom was not even fifty years old when I arrived there, and it was — is — very close to its early tribal traditions.

Saudi Arabia may be wealthy, but it is probably the least cultivated country in the rich and multifaceted Arab world, with the most simplistic and brutal conception of social relationships. Families are headed by patriarchs, and obedience to the patriarch is absolute. The only values that count in Saudi Arabia are loyalty and submission — first to Islam, then to the clan.

Yeslam's father, Sheikh Mohamed, was, in many ways, the archetype of the Saudi patriarch, though in fact he was born in neighbouring Yemen. His personality was larger than life; his will was law. Sheikh

Mohamed was a poor worker who had come to Saudi Arabia in the 1930s. He had a mind like fire for figures, though he couldn't read or write. Pious, honourable and scrupulous, and respected by his workforce, Sheikh Mohamed had built a company that grew into one of the largest construction groups in the Middle East, before he died in a plane crash, in 1967 at the age of fifty-nine.

Sheikh Mohamed's relationship with the Saudi royal family dated from the years when King Abdel Aziz, the founder of the Kingdom, was still on the throne. According to a Bin Laden family legend, the ailing King was unable to climb the stairs in one of his palaces, so Sheikh Mohamed's crew designed and installed a special ramp so that the King could be driven by automobile directly up to the second floor.

In another family story, my father-in-law drastically underbid an Italian company which was scheduled to construct the road from Jeddah to hilly Taef, where King Abdel Aziz often spent the summer months. Sheikh Mohamed followed a mule making the journey, mapped out the animal's trail, and used that path to build the road.

Yeslam's father was a generous man, given to great gestures of abundance. Once, I was told, when King Saud was on the throne,

Sheikh Mohamed had reached into his own deep pockets and paid the salaries of the government's civil servants to save the Kingdom from financial embarrassment. Another time, a group of poor Indonesians making a pilgrimage to Mecca were left stranded by their guide, without their return tickets or cash. They went to Sheikh Mohamed — the biggest employer in the region — to beg for work, so they could make enough to pay for the air fare home. He simply gave them the money.

Sheikh Mohamed was wily and brave. He often worked alongside his workforce; unlike most wealthy Saudis, he was not averse to manual labour, and willingly endured great hardship. Although I've no idea if the story is true, Yeslam told me that once, during the war between Egypt and Yemen in the 1950s, Sheikh Mohamed and his men had worked under fire from the Egyptian air force to complete construction of an airbase in a neighbouring region of Saudi Arabia.

This was life on a spectacularly grand scale, and Sheikh Mohamed carried that sense of the spectacular into his home life, too. Islam permits a man to marry four wives, and most Saudis are content to marry one or two — four at most. But, like a few of the royal princes, Sheikh Mohamed swelled the ranks of his wives by divorcing older women and marrying new ones as the whim took him. (Divorce is a simple procedure in Islam — for a man.) When he died, he had amassed twenty-two wives — twenty-one of them still living. I heard that on the night he died, Sheikh Mohamed had been planning to marry a twenty-third wife. He was headed there when his private plane crashed in the desert.

Sheikh Mohamed never actually lived at Kilometre Seven. He lived with most of his wives and children in a huge compound in Jeddah, and maintained smaller establishments in Riyadh and elsewhere. His favourite wife, Om Haidar, lived with him in the big house in Jeddah and he rotated nights as he pleased with other wives in smaller houses scattered around inside the high walls of his compound. Cooking and childcare were more or less collective, by affinity among the wives, and the current wives had a higher status than the divorced.

Sheikh Mohamed had had fifty-four children. I used to tease Yeslam, saying that his father had been competing with King Saud, who had over one hundred offspring. All Sheikh Mohamed's children would forever live their lives in the gigantic shadow of their father. To them, he was a hero — a distant, fabled figure, stern and deeply devout. The younger children rarely saw him. From time to time, Yeslam and his brothers would go to the big house for inspection. Their fearsome father would ask them if they had prayed, or ask them to recite the Koran, and reward them with a coin or a pat.

Sheikh Mohamed fascinated me. A poor, illiterate man from one of the most deprived regions on earth — the Hadramaut, in Yemen — he had emigrated to Saudi Arabia, a country bare of any elements of modern civilization. And he had become one of the most powerful men in the Kingdom's fledgling economy. Sheikh Mohamed became a kind of baron in that medieval regime. He was the largest employer in the country. He was befriended and trusted by kings. By any standard, in any culture, Sheikh Mohamed would have been counted a genius.

Sadly, none of his children has ever measured up to him. Yeslam came closest, with his sharp intelligence, but he was panicky and fearful. At the end of the day he didn't have the stature or the strategic vision of his father. Salem let the organization stagnate, and Bakr had no drive and was pedestrian. And Osama? Though he has certainly made the Bin Laden name famous across the world, I would like to believe that his father would not have approved of the way he did it.

Once, Yeslam told me, Tabet was caught out in a lie and Sheikh Mohamed hit him. Another time, he took one of his older sons to see King Faisal, who invited the child to come and sit at his side in his reception room. He insisted that the boy join him and designated a place where he should sit, but Sheikh Mohamed said no. He said no to the King. While he lived, his sons never disobeyed him or became involved in disputes with each other. The line of authority was clear: Sheikh Mohamed's word was law.

Sheikh Mohamed was a handsome, energetic man. I still have an imposing portrait of him in my living room today. In his Saudi robes and dark glasses, he gives off panache, strength and intelligence. His children lived in awe of him — the wives did too. I rarely met a Saudi woman who was not afraid of her husband. Sheikh Mohamed was not violent, but he had total power over his wives. He could neglect them or, worse, divorce them. They lived in confinement, utterly dependent on him. A wife cannot do anything without her husband's permission. She cannot go out or study, often cannot even eat at his table. Women must live in obedience, in isolation, and in fear that they may be cast out and summarily divorced.

Haidar's mother, the favourite wife, was still living near Kilometre Seven. She was a pretty woman and a very efficient organizer. With her, Yeslam said, the house was assured smooth functioning, and his father could relax. Om Haidar was more sophisticated than some of Sheikh Mohamed's other wives. She was Syrian and she had great poise. She smiled gently, her voice was melodious, and I believe that Om Yeslam consciously modelled herself on her.

But Om Haidar was not the ruler of the clan. All my mothers-in-law seemed to maintain relationships of perfect harmony with each other, although a few lived in Riyadh and Mecca, and several of the foreign-born wives — those who came from Lebanon, Egypt, or Ethiopia — moved back and forth between their homelands and Jeddah, where their children lived. Even Salem, the eldest brother, did not seem to issue edicts or rulings, although he was acknowledged as the clan leader, and many of my sisters-in-law, particularly those who had no brothers, depended on him for every major decision about their lives. There was a kind of common, unspoken understanding which ran the family machine without any one driver taking control.

By the time I arrived, seven years after Sheikh Mohamed's death, there were no apparent distinctions between current wives and those who had been divorced. Sheikh Mohamed had, of course, divorced many of them; and one, Om Ali, he remarried. His custom was to maintain his divorced wives and their children on his compound, so long as the women did not remarry, as the law permitted them to. If they did, like Om Tareg, he kept the children with him, distributing them among his other wives.

I learned that, in addition to maintaining wives and divorced wives, Sheikh Mohamed sometimes chose to establish contracts with semi-wives. The practice of *serah* — what we would call concubines, though the word is not a perfect equivalent — is not well-regarded in Saudi Arabia, and it is something you encounter rather rarely, but it has always been legal. Probably because in Islam no child may be illegitimate, it was long ago established that a man could set up a contract with a girl, or her father, for a kind of limited marital arrangement. The marriage lasts an hour or a lifetime, according to the contract. Whatever the relationship, the semi-wife does not inherit wealth on the man's death.

Sheikh Mohamed installed these mothers also on his compound and treated their children exactly as he did the others. If he cast one of these women out, for whatever reason, he always kept the child. In Saudi Arabia, the head of the family — be that the father or the eldest son — can demand the strictest application of the shariah Islamic law against a member of the clan. It chilled me whenever I saw it put to use. Over the years, I met many women who had been completely forbidden from having any contact with their children, even by phone. As I would learn, if a child flouts the harsh customs and conventions, the patriarch may even put that child to death.

8

Life as an Alien

Inevitably, as the months went by I began to settle into my new life. I started to think about the future. Musing about redecorating the house was a recurrent fantasy. I was enclosed there night and day, often for weeks at a time, and the decor was truly hideous.

I tried to keep myself busy by reading and playing with Wafah. One day, Yeslam's younger brother Osama came to visit. Today, of course, he is by far the most notorious of Yeslam's brothers. Back then, however, he was a minor figure, a young student attending King Abdel Aziz University in Jeddah, respected in the family for his stern religious beliefs, and recently married to a Syrian niece of his mother's.

Osama was perfectly integrated into the family, although he didn't live at Kilometre Seven. He was a tall man, despite the slightness of his build, and he had a commanding presence — when Osama stepped into the room, you felt it. But he was not strikingly different from the other brothers, just younger and more reserved. That afternoon I was playing with Wafah in the hallway when the doorbell rang. I, stupidly, automatically, answered it myself, instead of calling for the houseboy.

Catching sight of Osama and Aïsha's son Mafouz, I smiled and asked them in. 'Yeslam is here,' I assured them, but Osama snapped his head away when he saw me and glared back towards the gate. 'No, really,' I insisted. 'Come in.' Osama was making rapid back-off gestures with his hand, waving me aside and muttering something in Arabic, but I truly didn't understand what he meant. Mafouz could see that I was seemingly lacking in the basics of social etiquette, and he finally explained that Osama could not see my naked face.

In Saudi culture, any man who might one day become your husband is not supposed to see you unveiled. The only men who may look at you are your father, brother and husband, or step-father. Osama was among those men who followed the rule strictly. So I retreated into a back room while my admirably devout brother-in-law visited my husband. I felt stupid and awkward.

Years later, I was amazed to read in the Western press that Osama had been a playboy as a teenager in Beirut. I think if it were true, I would have heard about it. Another brother-in-law did have that reputation and had chased many a skirt while studying in Lebanon, but later he changed, and became a strictly religious man. I never heard such tales about Osama, however. The now-famous photographs that were taken of a crowd of teenaged Bin Laden brothers in Sweden don't show Osama. At the time, I think he was in Syria. The boy identified in the media as Osama is in fact another brother. As far as I know, Osama was always devout. His family revered him for his piety. Never once did I hear anyone murmur that his fervour might be a little excessive, or perhaps a passing phase.

The Bin Ladens were all religious, though their piety varied in degree. Men like Osama and Mahrouz were the most extreme. Bakr was devout, but not repressive. Like many young Saudi men, Yeslam, Salem and another brother, Hassan, were more casual about their practice of Islam, although as they got older, religion seemed to catch up with them.

The Bin Laden men could choose to be a little more flexible about their religious observance, but this right did not extend to the women. All the women in the Bin Laden family were very proper, and in Saudi Arabia that meant they were devout. When Yeslam's brother Hassan married a Lebanese girl, there was widespread gossip about her former job as an airline hostess. Leila confided in me that she felt her mother-in-law would never accept her. She suffered from the disapproval of the family.

I sought to please. I couldn't rid myself of the awareness of how disappointed Om Yeslam must have been that her son had married a foreigner. I tried to moderate my impetuous temperament. I tried to learn to pray: the ritual washing; wrapping every inch of myself in a light sheet; performing the ballet of kneeling, bowing and standing while facing Mecca, but I could never manage to pray five times a day, as most of the other Bin Laden women did.

The Bin Ladens were deeply proud of the Mecca shrine, like all Saudis. They are steeped from childhood in the honour and responsibility of caring for Mecca, where the Prophet Muhammad was inspired by Allah. And the Saudi form of Islam is the strictest — they would say purest — form that religion can take. In the 1700s an itinerant preacher called Sheikh Muhammad ibn Abd-al Wahhab — a kind of Muslim puritan revivalist — became inspired by his revulsion at the people's mixture of Islam with old prayers to sacred stones and trees, and their shrines to holy men. Abdel Aziz ibn Saud, then a desert warlord, was inspired by Sheikh Wahhab to conquer and unify the whole of Saudi Arabia in 1932.

This is how Saudi Arabia became the only country in the world to take the name of its ruling kings, the al-Sauds. They established Saudi Arabia — with some help from the British — wielding the sword and the Word. Their control of a vast country of separate Bedouin tribes was cemented by imposing absolute obedience to Sheikh Wahhab's strict Koranic rules, in order to preserve the holiness of Mecca.

Mohamed Bin Laden was so pious, and so beloved by the King, that his company, the Bin Laden Organization, was given the exclusive right to renovate Mecca and Medina, Islam's second holiest city. It is hard to convey the honour that this reflected on his family. It was no wonder that his wives were so religious, though sometimes it was hard for me to bear.

I went to Mecca for the first time with a female acquaintance of Kuwaiti origin. On the road, we passed huge billboards warning non-Muslims to turn back. We came to an inspection post: Saudi officials are obsessive about forbidding non-Muslims to soil the

Mecca holy sites. It made me nervous. My mother was born a Muslim, but her practice of Islam was certainly questionable in the light of the Bin Ladens' piety. And my father had been a Christian, something I never hid, but always felt I should. I had learned how to pray, certainly, but I didn't really feel I was a proper Muslim. Still, Abdou drove us through, cheerfully — 'Bin Laden' was all he said to the inspection official, and of course that was enough. We arrived just as the cry to prayer rang out, and I started nervously performing the prayer ritual.

An official from the terrifying religious police, the *mutawa*, immediately began yelling at me and I panicked. Had I made some crucial error in the ritual — something that betrayed my inexperience? Would I be disowned as an impostor? But Abdou told me it was because I was praying in the men's area. It hadn't even occurred to me that we would be kept separate, even here. Nothing comes easily, I thought, trying to breathe through my sudden fear.

We went a little farther along, to the section of the huge courtyard that is reserved for women. We prayed. We walked the seven turns, and drank the waters of the Zamzam, where three millennia ago Abraham's second wife, Hagar, was directed by God to find water for her young son Ishmael, father of the Arabs. We touched the Kaaba, the black stone that God gave Abraham, which so many millions of hands had touched before ours. We saw the locked door that led to the closed room which is the holy place within the holy place — a room where Yeslam and other Bin Laden men had been permitted to pray.

Philosophically, I have always felt that it doesn't matter how you pray to God or what texts you read — the Bible, the Koran, the Torah. But in that colossal, holy place of tradition, towards which one billion Muslims turn in prayer every day, even I felt a spiritual charge. I went home thoughtful. I was greeted by Yeslam's unbounded delight. It was not the sacred haj period, but I had accomplished the *umra*, the lesser pilgrimage to Mecca, without the millions of pilgrims who converge on the city during haj time. 'I've told everyone that you have done the *umra!*' he crowed. He seemed so proud of me. When I told him about the *mutawa*, he started laughing.

We started going out occasionally, socializing with other couples. Some of them were among the expatriate bankers and industrialists who had begun arriving en masse in Saudi Arabia to take part in the great boom. One or two were modern-thinking Saudis, who could bear to see an unveiled woman's face, and, more shocking still, dine with her at table. I felt inspired by these moments of normality, though I would almost always discover that these were not truly Saudi households — the wives were invariably from elsewhere, Syria or Egypt or Lebanon.

After one such dinner, on our late drive home, Yeslam gestured me to sit with him in the front. And then he said I could take the gauze off my face, if I wished. I sat there watching the street lights clearly, unveiled outside for the first time. It felt like another milestone. I needed to count these little victories. I clutched at these small signals of change. I felt they were carrying me forwards. I realize now that the bars of my cage were only moving a little wider apart, but at the time it seemed as if the door to freedom and choice was starting to creak open.

Sometimes it all seemed to be moving so slowly, and I would be overcome with despair. And yet I stayed, always. I realized that in some sense I was privileged. I was living a unique moment in the evolution of the country. Saudi Arabia was speeding away from the Middle Ages and making huge leaps ahead in material progress. Naively, I believed that economic change would be followed by social shifts too, which would alter beyond recognition the lot of Saudi women. I thought I could participate in that essential moment in history. I was at the crucial place, at the crucial time. The prospect of being part of the tremendous social changes which I believed were on the way was thrilling.

And yet nothing seemed to change for the women in the Bin Laden family. I felt the Bin Laden women were kept like pets by their husbands. All day long they waited for their husbands to come back — all night long too, sometimes, and when they did, the wives would perform their role as joyful, welcoming companions. They were kept shut in their homes, or occasionally accompanied out on special outings. Sometimes they were taken out, mostly to each other's houses. Preparing these little parties was the women's only occupation; that and the elaborate preening and fussing with their formal, frilly clothes that happened beforehand. Every tea party was the same. We seated ourselves stiffly on uncomfortable chairs. There was no small talk or deeper discussion, just a lot of silence, and little cups of tea and coffee with different kinds of cakes. Any talk centred on our children — who meanwhile spent most of their time with foreign maids — and on the Koran. Sometimes we talked about clothes.

I had the impression that none of the

women ever read, except perhaps the Koran and other works of Koranic interpretation. I never once saw one of my sisters-in-law pick up a book. These women never met with men other than their husbands, and never talked about larger issues even with the men they had married. They had nothing to say. We talked about the health of our husbands and children, and they made constant, quite kindly efforts to make a good Muslim out of me. As time went on, I did come to see the presence of some of them as a welcome distraction. Mostly, though, they bored me absolutely rigid.

Yeslam did not treat me as his brothers did their wives. If he had, I could not have borne living in Saudi Arabia. But in those days my husband was very different from other Saudi men. He treated me like a Western man would, more or less as his equal. Yeslam involved me in his life and thoughts. He enjoyed my intellect, and he sought my advice. We talked about everything, all the time. He wanted me to be his partner, a full member of a two-person team.

It became a kind of ritual. We would talk together while Yeslam showered, after he came home from work, around 2.00 or 3.00. We talked about his day, what I'd been reading, things on the news — it seemed we never stopped talking. We spent afternoons and evenings deep in discussion. Often the subject was politics. On a daily basis, Yeslam confided in me his troubles at the Bin Laden Organization, changes that he planned, or his worries for the company's future, the intrigues and the often nasty bickering and infighting of his apparently calm brothers.

Yeslam had a strange relationship with his brothers. On the one hand, they were his only companions — he had no male friends to speak of. His family members were the only people who counted in Yeslam's life. There is a Saudi saying, 'Me and my cousin against the stranger; me and my brother against my cousin.' Among nomads — and Saudi culture was formed by desert nomads — the clan is the only unit that makes sense. So Yeslam did trust his brothers more than most people in the West trust their family. He knew he could count on them to some extent. But with me, he could confide his frustrations with his clan — his brothers' petty squabbles, and their many hidden power struggles.

Sometimes I would look over at Yeslam, as we were playing cards or backgammon in the evening, or listening to music together, and I would catch my breath. He was so beautiful, with his fine features and gentle eyes. And he needed me. I knew he loved me. To him I was his force, his equal, a completely loyal partner who put her self aside in order that he could progress. But I was very young then, and I believed things would change. I lived for Yeslam and Wafah, and I lived for the future. I still thought that with Yeslam's intelligence and his family's power, we could help change things. I clutched at every sign that Saudi Arabia was entering the modern world: a lifted veil seen on the street; a new, women-only bank that meant women could have their own bank accounts; an English-language TV channel, or a new bookstore.

I was almost always disappointed. The English-language TV channel was censored to shreds. Apart from news of the King's latest foreign visit, it mostly showed cartoons and the cop show *Columbo* — shows with no kissing or politics. The bookstore sold almost no books: Saudi Arabian customs officials would not permit entry for any love stories, books by Jews or most books on religion, Middle Eastern politics or Israel. It was dispiriting, but again I assumed it was just a matter of time before things would change.

Meanwhile, I was beginning to make real friendships, and that helped. Salem's younger brother, Bakr, had moved into Salem's former house, just across the road from our own. Bakr himself was rather aloof, polite and pleasant, but always heavily aware of his high rank in the Bin Laden family. I knew Yeslam didn't like him much, but Bakr's wife, Haifa, was a delightful, bubbly woman, a blonde, blue-eyed Syrian with two sons. Haifa and I shared a sense of humour and her two young sons were a few years older than Wafah. She and Bakr had lived in Miami for a while. She spoke English and understood my claustrophobia, but she had moved to Saudi Arabia years before me, and because of her Arab background she melded into the Bin Laden family far more deftly than I ever could.

Haifa was different from me, but she was a kind of ally — my Arab counterpart. She was open-minded, lively and friendly, and I was grateful for that. Haifa was also a gifted mimic. She imitated to perfection one mother-in-law's waddle and my own lopsided gait, with high heels and handbag under a half-askew *abaya*. She was fun.

I think that I was a relief for Haifa too. Coming from the freer atmosphere of Syria, she struggled with the strict monotony of Saudi Arabia as I did. Safe in Haifa's garden, tanning by her pool, we howled with laughter at how depraved the mothers-in-law would think us if they caught sight of our swimsuits. We paddled together with our children. And it was Haifa who taught me, much more even than Yeslam, about the etiquette I should follow, and the various marriages and funerals and events I must, as a Bin Laden wife, attend.

The first time I took the decision to walk to her house across the street — the first time I turned up at Haifa's house *on foot*, having crossed the few metres of road *by myself*, instead of calling for my driver — Haifa grinned wildly. 'Carmen!' she cried. 'The revolution! Tomorrow all the Bin Ladens will be saying, 'We saw Carmen *on the street!*' '

Haifa loved her husband. It was not a completely arranged marriage: they had met in Syria and there was affection between them — something I rarely perceived in Bin Laden couples. In 1978, Haifa gave birth to her third child, a girl. I went to congratulate her a day later, just as Bakr arrived with their two sons. He told them, 'Kiss your mother's hand. She has given you a little sister.' It was formal, but it was sweet. It showed respect, I thought. There was real love in that marriage — it was one of the few marriages I saw in Saudi Arabia where that was true.

I became pregnant again. I was overjoyed, and I felt that Yeslam was too. A companion for Wafah — another baby — and surely this time we would have a boy. The whole Bin Laden clan seemed so happy to hear our news: I was greeted everywhere with cries of *'Inshallah*, you will have a boy!' The baby was due in June 1977, and I flew to Geneva a couple of months beforehand to be sure I was properly cared for.

The Bin Laden family had the right to use the special royal family suites in all the best Saudi hospitals, but I didn't really trust the doctors there. Most of them were trained in Syria and Egypt, and they seemed far too ready to pump you full of pills and injections. The other Bin Laden women usually gave birth in Jeddah, but for special check ups they often went abroad, to Europe or the United States. A large portion of our travelling time overseas was always taken up by medical visits.

My mother and sisters took care of me in the last few weeks of my pregnancy. I rested in the mild spring sunlight and watched Wafah playing in my mother's garden, just as I once had, so many years before. I could tell Wafah felt at ease in my mother's home, and Yeslam visited us frequently. It was a gentle period, one I would often look back to in the hard years to come.

Longing for a boy was not just a whim that occupied me in those last weeks of pregnancy. For Saudi women, it is essential to produce male heirs. It is not just a question of your personal status in society (though for many women that is part of the issue — to be called Om Ali sounds a lot better than plain Om Sarah). It can be a question of basic survival.

In the event of a husband's death, if his wife has only daughters, then they all become dependent on the husband's closest male relative even if they are adult. He is their guardian, and must approve the most simple of decisions, such as travel, education or the choice of a husband. In terms of inheritance, a family with only women is discriminated against. When the husband dies, if he leaves only daughters, then fifty per cent of his inheritance reverts to his parents and siblings. Only if the wife has sons does the entire estate pass to her and her children. And, once he is an adult, the eldest son can act as guardian to his mother and sisters. *Inshallah*, I will have a boy.

At last, my contractions began, a little ahead of schedule. Before heading for the clinic to give birth, I phoned Yeslam, who was still in Saudi Arabia. 'Can't you wait till tomorrow when my plane arrives?' he asked in a rather petulant tone. I had to laugh at him — he was so used to having his way. Did he think I could delay a baby's birth to accommodate his schedule?

The baby was a girl, a beautiful little girl.

She was perfect. I loved her instantly. We called her Najia, a name I always liked. It means the same as Yeslam — Protected. Najia was a delight. She was the easiest baby a mother could wish for. She added so much to my life. She was so sweet and fragile. And now that I knew better what lay in store for her, as a girl in Saudi Arabia, I did wish so much — for her sake — that she had been a boy.

I wondered sometimes, watching my children: if Yeslam had been a European man, would having two girls have been such an issue? Sensing my turmoil, Yeslam tried to comfort me. He insisted that it didn't matter, but something inside me told me differently. And I felt I had let him down.

If I'd had a son, I would have brought him up to know that women are equal to men. He would have protected his sisters if anything happened to Yeslam. With a boy, even without Yeslam's help, we would have a close defender with values I could relate to.

At the time, of course, I could not know this, but in a sense it was Najia who, years later, would save us all. If I had had a boy, it would have been easier to cope with Saudi ways. We were wealthy and respected; our lives were comfortable there. But because I had two little girls to care for, I would gradually become more sensitive to the dismal, oppressive conditioning that Saudi girls must suffer as they grow into women. With little Najia and Wafah in my care, I ultimately found myself compelled to save my daughters from that culture. I simply could not watch my precious daughters submit to Saudi customs. So Najia was heaven-sent. Not only was she delightful, but subsequently she gave me the strength I would need to deliver us all from Saudi Arabia.

9

Two Mothers, Two Babies

We headed back to Saudi Arabia that August. It was steaming hot, and a group of the Bin Laden brothers made plans for a day trip to the family country house in Taef, in the mountains, about two hours' drive from Jeddah. This was a vast house, built in the 1950s or 60s, devoid of any special charm, but it was a little cooler there, and it made for a change of routine. We women established ourselves in the female quarters with the children.

My little Najia was a few months old, and Osama's wife, Najwah, had a son, Abdallah, who was about the same age. Abdallah commenced howling, and kept it up for hours. He was thirsty and Najwah kept trying to feed him water with a teaspoon, but it was obvious he was far too small to manage to drink properly from a spoon. Najia was gulping water from her baby bottle constantly and I offered it to Najwah.

'Take it, he's thirsty,' I told her, but Najwah

105

wouldn't take the bottle. She was almost crying herself. 'He doesn't want the water,' she kept saying. 'He won't take the spoon.' Om Yeslam had to explain to me that Osama didn't want the baby to use a bottle. There was simply nothing Najwah could do about it. She was so sad, and so powerless — a drab little figure, very young, cradling her baby in the fold of her arm, watching him in such obvious distress. I couldn't stand it.

It was punishingly hot outside, perhaps a hundred degrees, and a baby can dehydrate in a few hours at such temperatures. I couldn't believe someone would really let his tiny child suffer so much over some ridiculous dogmatic idea about a rubber teat. I couldn't just sit there and watch this happen. Surely Yeslam could do something. I couldn't go over to the men's side of the house to appeal to him to intercede, but a sister could. I begged one of them to get Yeslam.

When Yeslam arrived, I railed at him. 'Go and tell your brother that his child is suffering,' I said. 'The baby needs a bottle. This has to stop.' But Yeslam came back shaking his head. He told me, 'It's no use. This is Osama.' I just could not believe it. All the way back to Jeddah it haunted me. Osama could do as he wished with his wife and child:

that was a given. His wife didn't dare disobey him: this was a given, too. Worse still, nobody would dare to intercede. Even Yeslam seemed to agree that Osama's rule over his household should be absolute. The force and command I had once seen in Yeslam, and admired, seemed to be dissipating in the hot Arabian air.

As Yeslam drove back down the hills, I sat in silence, veiled, my fists clenched, staring at the empty world outside. I felt suffocated. I'm sure Osama would not have wanted to lose his baby. It was not as if he didn't care about the child, but the baby's suffering was less important than a principle which he probably imagined stemmed from some seventh-century verse in the Koran. And his family was simply awed by Osama's zeal and intimidated into silence. For them, as for most Saudis, you simply could not be too excessive about your religious beliefs.

That is when I realized just how powerless I had become. If Yeslam were not there, and if I did not have a son to take on that role, my guardian — and the guardian of my daughters — would be one of Yeslam's brothers. I would be dependent for everything on that man. Men like Osama could one day rule over me and my children. There would be nothing whatsoever that I could do about it.

All that long drive back to town, I thought about the mothers I knew who were forced to live without their children. It was a litany of women who had no control over their lives — who had no recourse. There was Taiba, one of Yeslam's sisters, a tragic figure. Her husband had divorced her and kept their two small daughters — they were aged four and seven when we first met. Taiba was permitted to see them only on Friday afternoons. Om Yeslam said the children cried bitterly every time Taiba had to leave them. She was a sad, faded woman — old, somehow, and worn, though she must have been well under 30.

One dear friend of mine, who was Swedish, had previously been married to a Saudi, then divorced. She had planned to keep her two year-old son with her, but one afternoon in Beirut, at the tailor's, my friend let go of her son's hand. A few minutes later, he was gone — kidnapped by his Saudi father. She never saw him again, though she begged for just one visit.

Najia, another of Yeslam's sisters, married her husband just before I arrived in Saudi Arabia. After he divorced her, she never saw her four children. I would implore her, 'Why don't your brothers do something about it?'

and Najia would just smile at me, 'Ah, Carmen,' as if I was some kind of village idiot. You could never say an ill word about the brothers, and a husband's rule could not be questioned.

It ate at me. I felt a heavy weight inside. What if Yeslam had an accident right then, driving back to Jeddah? What if he were no longer there to protect my small, now bitter-tasting, freedoms? What would be my daughters' destinies, as Saudi women? Who would decide their lives? Would it be Salem? Bakr? Ibrahim? And who could say what those men would become, with age and power? I would be a kind of beggar, completely dependent on their whims, as they controlled my children's lives in every minor detail.

For the first time I felt a real gulf open between Yeslam and me, on a matter that meant more to me than anything else in the world. When I sought his reassurance, he seemed dismissive. I needed him to take steps to find a way to resolve the problem — some kind of plan, a road map that would guide me in case of a tragedy, to ensure that I would always be in charge of our girls, whatever life might have in store. I wanted him to tell me that he would always look after us, make sure we would always be safe from the whims of

109

those men. To me, a man protects his family, thinks ahead, and makes provision to keep them safe. But somehow it didn't concern him. Yeslam could not understand the depth of my fear. And when I finally grasped that, it made me even more afraid. Suddenly, I felt I was alone and I was completely powerless.

Nothing was ever the same after that day in Taef. My hopes for a freer world in the future, where women would at least be able to have a say in their children's lives, were forever shattered and buried in the Arabian desert sand by the dogmatic Wahhabi perception of Islam. Emotionally, the fear and loneliness I felt then coloured everything I was to see and live through in the years to come. Although I tried to behave as though everything was normal, a constant worried feeling now accompanied me everywhere. I was no longer a carefree mum. The future had a bitter taste to it now.

10

My Own Chief Inmate

I tried to put my panic behind me, although it remained at the back of my mind as long as I lived in Saudi Arabia. I had to get on with my life. I distracted myself with a longed-for new project. Om Yeslam and Fawzia had decided to move out, and Yeslam had given them a parcel of land adjoining ours for their own house. Now that Yeslam and I had two little girls, we were a real family, and I could try to make us all a real home — a home of our own.

I hired a cook as I had no desire to work in my kitchen as Om Yeslam did, and made plans to knock down walls and open out our gloomy, ill-designed rooms. I designed a new kitchen adjoining the house, put in big panels of sliding glass to open out the living room, and had new quarters built for the two female servants.

By this time I had begun speaking directly to our male servants — the houseboy, the cook, the gardener, the doorman, and our two drivers. They lived in a separate lodging beside the gate. One afternoon I found the interphone wasn't functioning and went out to their quarters to call Abdou, my driver. Poking my head around the door, I found a scene of such squalor that I could not help investigating further. As the servants were watching a football match at Bakr's servants' quarters, I asked Abdou to stand at the door and make sure no one followed me. I couldn't risk being found alone with one of the male servants in their bedroom. As I rapidly inspected their quarters, I discovered a kitchen that was unbelievably dirty and smelled foul; the walls were black with grime. Even the bedrooms were filthy.

It was my property, but I felt almost as if I was trespassing. No woman had ever been inside that lodging. The men who lived there went home to see their wives and families perhaps once every two years. They scorned what they considered women's work, and though they had to clean my home, they lived in their own rooms almost like animals. I was horrified by what I had stumbled upon, inside the walls of my own compound. I made Abdou buy paint and gave the men money for new furniture; I insisted that they clean up.

Meanwhile, I got on with redecorating our house. It was a relief, but I had not foreseen the extent of the challenge. Shopping for furnishings was almost impossible: there were no shops. Finally, I discovered that one Lebanese woman married to a Saudi had set up a kind of furniture store on the first floor of her villa, filled with modern furniture she purchased in Europe. It was an odd sort of shop — half-home, half-warehouse — but I did at least manage to pick out new, thick, cream carpeting. The nasty dark green wall-to-wall had to go.

How to carpet the house, though? Because I could not be seen or spoken to by the male workers, I had to assume that they knew their craft, and rely on Yeslam's Egyptian male secretary to direct them. I resigned myself to this obvious waste of his time and energy, briefed him, and when the team of workers arrived, I agreed to retreat to a back room for the entire day. It was dusty, it was noisy, and the children were tetchy, and that evening, when I emerged, my eyes met a shambles. The carpet had been laid at right angles to our big new windows, so that every seam was clearly visible. It looked no better than the shoddy old green one.

I told Yeslam the work would have to be redone. He sighed, and next morning instructed the workers to tear it up and replace it. Next day, we returned to our

113

cloister. Next night, the carpet seams were less obvious, but a flawed piece had been laid right in the middle of the floor, exactly where it would be most visible. I certainly didn't want to live for years with this obvious mistake. So I told Yeslam it would have to be redone again. I'm not sure Yeslam even knew what I was talking about. Certainly he was frustrated. He had plenty of better things to do, and he found the whole rigmarole almost as tiresome as I did. So he just said, 'Go. Tell them yourself.'

This was truly a gigantic step. For a Bin Laden to talk to a male worker — an outsider, not even a household servant, practically a stranger from the street — was unheard of. I cloaked myself in my *abaya*, but did not veil my face — I needed to see properly. And then I emerged from my back room to see the workers and tell them what to do, but they would not look at me. I told them to tear out the carpet again, but they would not listen to me. The Sudanese worker who was laying down the carpet simply laid down some more. I repeated myself and raised my voice. Finally, he turned his head slightly, still not facing me. 'I do not take orders from women,' he growled.

Only when Yeslam's secretary arrived and insisted repeatedly that I was in charge of the work and he should listen to what I said, did the carpet finally get laid. Later, in my bedroom, I boiled with frustration. I didn't know whether to laugh or cry. Every single gesture I wanted to make seemed to be under the control of a man. I had never in my life felt so dependent. But I soothed myself: life was changing. There was building all around us now. Jeddah had become a colossal building site that stretched towards us down the Mecca road. Donkey Square and its squalid, dark grocery stores was being transformed into Dome Square, with a huge, modern, public space that was quite beautiful. Every time I returned from a few weeks' stay in Geneva, I found I couldn't recognize parts of the city.

So, in a physical sense, Saudi Arabia had changed immensely. No country anywhere developed as suddenly as Saudi Arabia did in the first five or six years that I lived there. Half a century before, people had wrapped themselves in wet sheets at night to get cool enough to sleep; now, everyone seemed to have air-conditioning. There were car dealerships everywhere: at some, you could even part-trade camels for a new Toyota.

Awash with petrol-dollars, it seemed that the Saudis could not spend enough. The first fashion boutiques were sprouting up, staffed only by women, so you could remove your face-veil to look at the clothes, or even disrobe to try items on. Women indulged in shopping frenzies. Underneath their veils, the younger women were made up like movie-stars now, dressed in the latest European designs. Hairdressers still came to the house, though. Hair was a major preoccupation, hidden away, then erotically revealed only to husbands. We continued to live in almost complete seclusion from the world of men.

Stores brimmed with the accessories of the modern world such as electronic gadgets and expensive sneakers. Suddenly a Safeway supermarket leapt up downtown, and it became the height of excitement to go shopping there. I was the only Bin Laden woman who dared go out alone with my driver, though — the others always took friends, or at least a maid. It was a social occasion. From time to time, you might even see a husband and wife shopping together. Now, every modern product could be bought — and was. We filled trolley after trolley with Jell-O, Campbell's soup, Swiss cheeses and chocolates. Bread from the bakery still came peppered with weevils — I insisted my cook learn to bake bread — but now we had pineapple chunks and real milk. They tasted of progress.

Carmen, aged six, on holiday in Persia, now Iran
'I was brought up in Switzerland but spent my holidays in Persia, visiting my mother's family.'

Carmen, aged 14
'My mother was a stickler for appearances and until I rebelled she used to dress all four of us girls exactly alike'

In my mother's garden in Geneva in 1973
*'The summer I met Yeslam, young people ruled the world. I was
excited about my future and very much in love.'*

My sisters Magnolia, Salomé and Béatrice with our
maternal aunt and her two children in Geneva

Yeslam's brother Ibrahim and their father Sheikh Mohamed in Jeddah in the 1950s
'Sheikh Mohamed had fifty-four children in all. He was a formidable man and I still keep a photo of him in my living room in Geneva.'

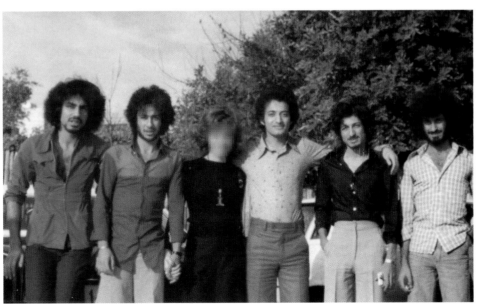

Some of Yeslam's family on a trip to the Pacific Palisades. Ahmad, Shafik, Regaih, Yahla, Yeslam and Ahmad.
'With their jeans and their Afro hair, they looked just like any American – on the outside.'

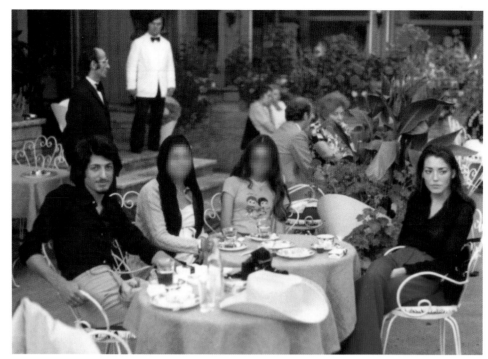

At tea with Yeslam, his mother Om Yeslam and his sister
Fawzia in Interlaken, Switzerland in 1973
'More and more Yeslam included me in his family outings.'

*'Saudi women did not
have photos in their
passports, but as a
foreigner I needed one for
my visa. My face had to
be visible, but naturally I
wore the headscarf.'*

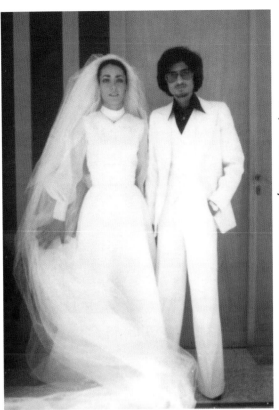

Jeddah, in 1974
'Since cameras were very unusual in Saudi Arabia at the time, I have only a few amateurish snapshots of the actual event. So, the following day, we took some shots. Whereas the day before Yeslam had been in full traditional costume, here he is wearing a western suit.'

Yeslam and his brother Ibrahim, the day after the wedding celebration
'It was rare to have so many flowers in Jeddah at the time.'

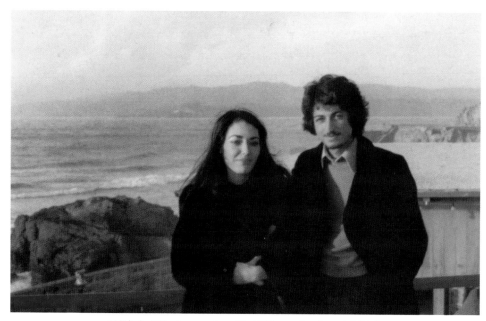

With Yeslam in California in 1974
'It was our first trip to the States. America was like a dream
come true for me, incredibly open, truly a land of opportunity.'

With Yeslam, Fawzia, Om Yeslam, Mary Martha and
Wafah in Santa Monica in 1976
'Yeslam bought a little Mooney single-engine plane.
I took flying lessons.'

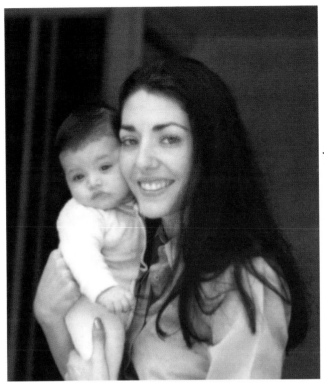

With three-month-old Wafah
'The birth of my first little girl was the most momentous event of my life. It changed me completely as a person.'

Mary Martha with Wafah on her first birthday
'Mary Martha has been my dearest friend, my mentor and a constant source of inspiration and comfort. I called her my American mum.'

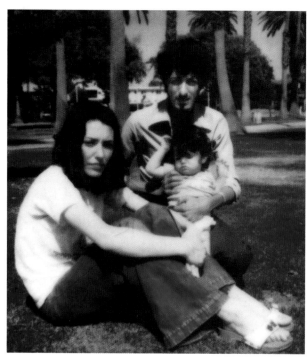

With Wafah and
Yeslam in Santa
Monica in 1976
*'I was so happy with
my beautiful baby
and my clever
handsome husband.
Life seemed full of
possibility.'*

On Yeslam's
graduation day at the
University of Southern
California in 1976
*'I had encouraged
Yeslam to study and
even though I had to
give up school myself,
I was thrilled when he
graduated.'*

In our garden in Jeddah, with Yeslam, my mother-in-law,
Wafah and Najia
*'I had two babies now and we were a real little family, but the
emotional loneliness I had experienced after that terrible day at
Taef had not left me.'*

Swimming with Najia in Haifa's pool
*'Haifa was a great friend to me. We kept in touch long after I
left Saudi Arabia, but after Nine Eleven I never saw her again.'*

With my mother and Yeslam in Geneva one December

'We spent many Christmases in Geneva. It didn't seem to bother Yeslam that we marked such a Christian holiday, although later it became difficult for me to celebrate even my own children's birthdays.'

'A family Christmas, unpacking presents with the girls.'

With Yeslam and Najia at our house in Jeddah
'In public I wore the abaya which covered my whole body. This photo of me partially uncovered could be taken in our house, but as soon as I left the gate I would have to adjust my abaya.'

Najia with some of the decorations that I made for the girls' birthday party in Jeddah
'It was important to me that not everything in their lives came from a shop. I spent hours making those swans.'

In our backyard
'In Jeddah, my girls could only play within the confines of the house. And even there our lives were increasingly restricted. As Saudi culture began to regress, our small freedoms slipped away.'

Fawzia and Majid's wedding in 1981. Khalil, Salem, Yeslam, Om Yeslam, Fawzia, Majid and his family
'We pulled out all the stops for Fawzia's wedding. I was very fond of Majid and devastated when he was killed in a tragic accident just five years later.'

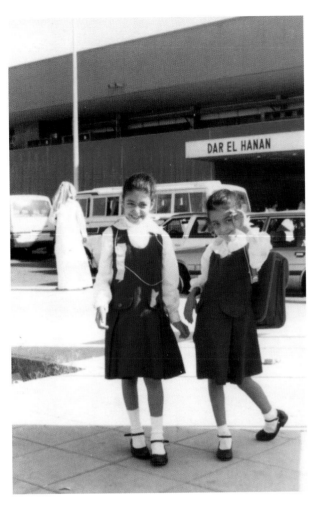

Wafah and Najia at school in Jeddah
'I was insistent that the girls should go to school, but worried by what they learned there.'

By the poolside in Jeddah
'Of course, photos are a very private matter in Saudi Arabia, but I was keen to have some pictures of my daughters growing up, so I asked the official photographer of the Bin Laden Organization to come to the house.'

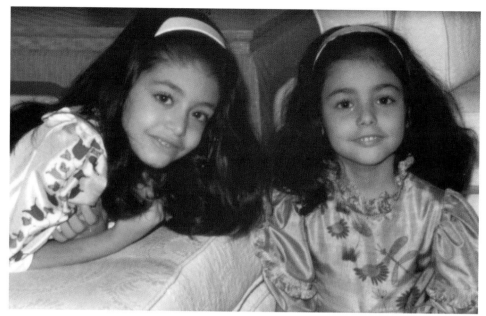

Wafah and Najia in Jeddah

In Jeddah on our last trip
'As the girls were growing up, Yeslam's behaviour began to change. In a restrictive society he had allowed us small liberties, but in a free country he became more and more closed.'

Noor, who has never set foot in Saudi Arabia

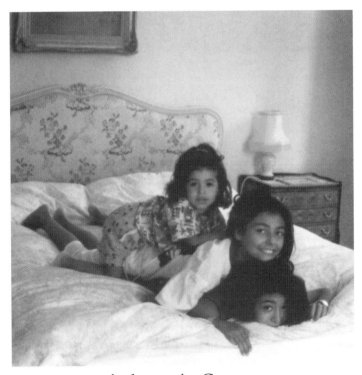

At home in Geneva
'This was the real beginning of freedom. Slowly, we all got used to living our lives without the constant fear of transgression.'

'After Nine Eleven, our private lives became public and I felt that I had to let the world know where we stand.'

'Despite the years of struggle, my consolation is that I know now that my beautiful girls are free to be who they want to be.'

By now I was used to my cumbersome *abaya*, but it still occasionally betrayed me. One day I was shopping, accompanied by my driver, Abdou, when I tripped over the black cloth. I tumbled down the stairs and somehow managed to roll myself up in its folds. I was trapped, like a mummy, completely unable to get up. I raised my head slightly and I could see Abdou, smiling in embarrassment. He didn't dare approach to help me up. I laughed too. I couldn't help but see the comedy of the situation, and clumsily made it back on my feet without his help.

The fever of consumerism infected even the staid Bin Laden women. Safeway was just the beginning; now, my sisters-in-law began redecorating too. But the furnishings they chose were loud and garish, terrible imitations of the objects I had carefully chosen. In Fawzia's house, everything was bright and shiny and mis-matched. She kept the plastic flowers. You could see the plumbing pipes in the bathroom; the workmanship was shoddy. Fawzia and the others never complimented me on my home, because they didn't think I was worthy of their admiration. They copied me, and yet they lorded it over me. It always came down to one thing: they were Saudis. I was not.

I read voraciously and I was developing

quite a library. I brought back crate-loads of books from Geneva. The dreaded customs officials were not bold enough to search Bin Laden luggage for literary contraband. I read politics, economics, biographies, philosophy — anything challenging that I could lay my hands on. One time I read a magazine article about female circumcision, the horrible practice of mutilating girls' genitals, which is still common in Egypt and other parts of Africa.

Om Yeslam was in the kitchen, and I was so upset by what I had read that I blurted it out to her. I suppose I wanted comfort. I certainly didn't expect the reaction I received. She smiled at me and said, 'It's not so bad, you know. An Egyptian woman comes, and it is just a little cut, such a little cut. The girl is very young. It doesn't hurt so very much.'

Was Om Yeslam among the women who had been so barbarically mutilated? Was Fawzia? Was Sheikh Mohamed's eldest daughter, Aïsha? How many of the family's wives and daughters carried this awful emotional and physical scar among all their other secrets? Was there no end to the pain that Saudi women had to bear? I ran to my little girls, and held them for a long time. My perfect little girls.

Slowly, as we began circulating a little

more, I began to feel the beginnings of social progress. Younger, more modern-thinking Saudis began to relax their observance of traditions. More and more women began to discard the veil. They walked through shopping malls, though rarely on the public streets, with the bare triangles of their faces exposed, although they still had to wear the *abaya*. Om Yeslam herself began keeping her veil off in front of her driver. She even began to speak to him directly.

Meanwhile, I vowed that I would be myself inside my own home. Life outside was far from normal, but I would run my household my way. It would be a refuge: my haven. I saw the servants as people, like myself, but in different circumstances, and I sought to understand them. I know that the servants liked me. I was polite and didn't bark orders like the other women. My children said please and thank you. Though I may have been demanding, I was never insulting. This was unusual, and widely remarked upon. The Bin Ladens saw their servants as objects — they functioned adequately, or they were stupid.

One time, after a sandstorm, I asked our elderly Pakistani doorman to clean the marble terrace we had installed outside the house. He took the new mop I had purchased, wet it, and began moving it around in circles. The result was muddy circles. I repeated my request; the result was the same. I admit I raised my voice — I was exasperated. I asked him what, exactly, he could not understand about this simple task. But then I stopped myself. What did this poor man know of mopping? He had lived most of his life with a beaten-earth floor. So I kicked off my sneakers, hiked up the legs of my trousers, and began to show him how to mop, in straight lines. Yeslam arrived just at that moment. '*What* are you doing?' he cried at me, infuriated. I hurried inside. I didn't know what was worse — displaying my ankles to a man, or mopping the floor. A Bin Laden woman does neither.

I found that incident rather amusing, but on other occasions I was somewhat less conciliatory. I once found Yeslam's Yemeni driver parked inside our compound, in front of our house, with the motor running. Even from a distance of a few metres I could feel the heat coming off the engine and could smell it burning. I said, 'Turn off the engine, it's going to overheat.' But Yeslam's driver ignored my order. 'I have to keep the air-conditioning on for Sheikh Yeslam,' he said. When I insisted, he replied, 'I don't take orders from women.' It was so insulting and absurd — the car was on the verge of bursting into flames! I yelled at him, 'When Sheikh Yeslam is not here, I'm the one in charge!' Bakr heard the commotion from his house across the street and came over to intervene. Needless to say, the driver immediately turned off the engine.

Life went on. We put in a tennis court. I so longed for exercise. Yeslam had learned to play in Los Angeles, and I ordered dozens of rackets and shoes in every size. We began inviting people for tennis parties on Thursday nights. This was another attempt to create a normal life. I would wear normal clothes and we would serve barbecued sirloin steaks and beer, just like in America. As alcohol was banned; it was a little tricky to buy it on the black market. But embassy personnel brought it in under diplomatic seal, and the drivers ran an underground commerce. Abdou, my driver, purchased beer from the chauffeurs of an African embassy. We were safe: the religious police never dared to inspect the homes of Princes or Bin Ladens.

I was the only woman in the family who received men at home. Haifa used to say, 'At least Yeslam comes home and spends time with you. He talks with you. He lets you live your life.' Haifa wasn't jealous. She was glad for me, pointing out ways in which Yeslam was special. She didn't want to brave the world in the same way that I seemed to need to. She was trying to help me to adjust to my Saudi life and to be happy.

My Thursday night parties did preserve my sanity, I think. Foreigners would come — embassy people, Western businessmen and a few Arabs working for multinational corporations, who had headed for the booming Gulf only to be crippled by their social isolation. The visiting businessmen, in particular, were infinitely grateful for a break from the dismal hotel rooms where they often waited for weeks to be received by some Prince or arrogant local businessman. Working in Saudi Arabia was so difficult for them: the endless waiting, the inactivity, all the restrictions.

Many expatriates living in Saudi Arabia were so desperate for amusement and escape, they brewed their own moonshine alcohol in their bathtubs. Once, at Safeway, I saw a huge crowd of them surrounding a display of chocolates, excitedly shoving dozens of boxes into each of their trolleys. Curious about what was going on, I examined one man's purchases in the check-out line. They were liqueur chocolates, with Kirsch! I had a good laugh at that. Some customs official had obviously slipped up.

Our Thursdays were open house — anything from twenty-five to seventy people would turn up. There were regulars, like the American ambassador, John West, and his wife Lois, friends who have stood by me to this day. Their daughter Shelton was about twenty years old. I could barely imagine how difficult Saudi life must have been for her, a young, single American girl in such a closed society.

In contrast, the atmosphere at our house was really relaxed, like the social events I'd so enjoyed in America. We set up a TV room for the children, with videos. People brought their friends. For the expats, these evenings became a real event in what passed for the Jeddah social calendar. The first time the wife of the Belgian ambassador came, she was resplendent in an elaborate long dress, and visibly startled to see me in Capri pants, alongside men wearing shorts. 'Wow, it really *is* casual!' she exclaimed. 'Every time somebody says 'casual' in this country I find everyone dressed to a T. This is so unexpected!'

The tennis was a distraction; it relaxed the atmosphere. Most of us talked. People came with the latest news. We talked about politics, or books. (My much-envied bookshelves were becoming a kind of community library.) Other times, the businessmen would talk about major contracts they were negotiating, and the expanding opportunities in the country.

These were the people who were building the new, modern Saudi Arabia. Talking with them, listening to them and having them listen back, became my lifeline. It was stimulating, a challenge. And the socializing was also good for Yeslam's business. When these men, often directors of major corporations, came to our home, it opened new doors for Yeslam. It made him different from other Saudis. It was quite something to be invited to Yeslam's house. He was becoming influential, and he was from the great Bin Laden family. And even within the hierarchy of Bin Laden brothers, Yeslam was rising to become a major player, someone to be reckoned with.

Sometimes Yeslam would invite Saudi men to these tennis parties, but no Saudi women ever came. I felt defiant about maintaining normality when Saudi men were around. I thought that if the men saw me speaking freely with Yeslam they would get used to it, and maybe realize how much richer and more worthwhile it was to have a relationship of exchange and companionship with your wife. I thought I was helping Saudi society evolve, but perhaps most Saudis found the casual atmosphere too threatening to handle.

Though Yeslam's brothers often dropped in, they never stayed.

One Thursday evening in 1978 all the diplomats were talking about the latest rumour that was racing through Jeddah. One of the King's young great-nieces, Princess Mish'al, had been cold-bloodedly murdered in a parking lot downtown. Barely an adult, Mish'al had been promised in marriage to a much older man. She had tried to flee the country with her lover, using another passport, but had been captured at the airport.

No woman can leave Saudi Arabia — or even travel outside the city she lives in — without the written permission of her husband or father, or son. A woman is never a legal adult. But there exists a women's underground network to trade passports and permissions, and because no customs official would dare ask a woman to unveil, it is not difficult to assume another identity.

Nonetheless, Mish'al had been caught and her grandfather, Prince Mohamed, the brother of King Khaled, had ordered her to be killed for bringing shame on her family. King Khaled had apparently resisted his brother's order, but Prince Mohamed had insisted and he was the patriarch of his clan. There was no trial and Mish'al was shot six times. A British man passing by had taken photos. Now, to the Saudi government's fury, the BBC was planning to broadcast a documentary.

I was rigid with horror and I thought about it for a long time. A grandfather could order his young granddaughter to be put to death because she had fallen in love; and nobody could prevent it. This was not even an Islamic issue. In some sense, it went deeper than that. There had been no trial by an Islamic court; no edict from the imams. The force at work in this dramatic, awful event was the old Bedouin culture of Saudi Arabia — savage, bitter customs that maintain their grip on society to this day.

As nomads, Bedouins travel light: the family is the anchor of the tribe. Women and camels are a Bedouin tribe's only possessions. Ruthlessness is a positive value in the desert. And honour, for reasons I cannot even begin to fathom, does not come from compassion or good works — it is focused on the absolute possession of women. Women are not free in any way — not even free to have emotions, such as love or longing. A disobedient woman dishonours her clan and is eliminated.

My first thought when I heard about Mish'al was for my innocent little girls. This could happen one day to Wafah or Najia. One

126

of their uncles might be perfectly capable of ordering his niece to be put to death, and I would be powerless. There are no words to describe my anger and my renewed panic that day. If our family trip to Taef had been my first wake-up call to the reality of Saudi Arabia, Mish'al's death was surely the second.

★ ★ ★

I decided to celebrate the joint birthdays of Wafah and Najia, in May. I had no idea how many religious quandaries would be raised by this simple and innocent decision. I just went ahead and phoned all the sisters-in-law to invite their children. My sister-in-law Rafah was particularly startled.

'We don't even mark the birthday of the Prophet Muhammad,' Rafah exclaimed. 'Christians mark birthdays. Christmas is a birthday.'

'What are you saying?' I replied, bewildered. 'This isn't some kind of idol-worship. I just want to show a little girl that I'm happy she was born. I'm saying, 'You were born that day, for me it was a happy day.' It isn't Christian.' I didn't convince her. For Rafah and the others, it was a matter of religion, and they were steadfast. In Saudi Arabia — for Bin Ladens — I learned that birthday celebrations are *haram*.

It may have been a trivial issue, but it annoyed me greatly. Rafah and the others were convinced they held the deeper truth. They saw the West as depraved, a decadent culture on the verge of collapse. It became important to me, perhaps excessively so. I didn't want to renounce everything about my culture to please the Bin Ladens. I was not going to deprive my children of something so basic as a birthday. Yeslam agreed to let me do it. It was not the first time we had braved tradition.

I decided to mark the day with another project: huge cut-out polystyrene figures that I would make with scissors and pins. They would be much more beautiful than store-bought decorations, and they would show my girls that not everything must be bought from a shop. I worked for weeks. Perhaps out of curiosity, several of the sisters-in-law came along with their children. They played and shrieked till late. It was like a fairy tale celebration.

But every year, as the children grew older, it got harder to persuade their mothers to permit them to attend. Despite my friendship with Haifa, I still felt alone. I was living in a society where women were nothing and wanted to be nothing. They didn't seem to seek the changes that I was expecting and longing for, and I felt frustrated, surrounded by women who didn't have the will or courage to resist. They had intelligence and energy, many of them, but they expressed it only in religion. They lived, but only for their faith, their personalities were completely annihilated.

I was mistress of my own house, now, but there were days when I also felt like its chief inmate. After the evening prayer call at dusk, I would stand on the marble terrace and listen to the thousands of birds that flew overhead, calling to each other as the huge, orange sun sank into the desert behind our house. They made an incredible racket, wheeling across the sand in black clouds, and there was almost nothing else to see for miles. It was beautiful, but it was always, always the same — stark, empty of imagination, creativity and real companionship. As the months went by, I found these silent vigils gave me a heavy, claustrophobic feeling. My girls were inside the house behind me, but my life sometimes felt as barren and empty as the sand.

11

The Brothers

As befitted his rank as the tenth son of Sheikh Mohamed, Yeslam occupied a rather junior position in the Bin Laden Organization during our first year in Saudi Arabia. To my delight, though, it soon became obvious to all that his talents were being wasted. Yeslam was far more intelligent and better educated than his brothers, and the company was doing less well than it appeared. They badly needed Yeslam's skills.

At the time, it was still being run by a board of eight trustees who had been appointed by King Faisal after Sheikh Mohamed died, to look after the interests of his young children, only two of whom had reached the age of twenty-one. The organization was among the largest in Saudi Arabia, and as such deserved special care. Moreover, Sheikh Mohamed had worked for King Faisal's father, the famed Abdel Aziz, and his brother, King Saud, building most of their palaces and helping out in other ways. He had a bond with the royal family.

The eight trustees, all fine, respectable older men, were deeply conservative and completely averse to taking risks. Other construction companies had begun growing alongside the stagnating Bin Laden Organization, some of them sponsored by powerful princes. It was said that these competitors were better connected than the Bin Ladens, and in Saudi Arabia, connections are your bottom line. Their competitors were aggressive and powerful, and were winning contracts left and right.

Meanwhile, there was also trouble among the brothers, namely Salem, Sheikh Mohamed's eldest son, and his second son, with another wife, Ali, whom I had met in Lebanon. When Sheikh Mohamed sent Salem away to be educated abroad, he decided to keep Ali in Saudi Arabia. When Sheikh Mohamed died, both Salem and Ali were legally adults, and Salem decided to take his rightful place as ruling male in the family and the corporation. Ali, who had stayed at his father's side, felt that he should be in charge.

For years Ali contested Salem's decisions, and the rivalry between them was doing the company no good. Finally, Ali petitioned King Faisal for permission to leave the Bin Laden Organization, and Saudi Arabia.

131

Although Ali's claim to be Sheikh Mohamed's true successor did have some merit, the King had to agree to his departure from the company. Even King Faisal could not permit the rule of the eldest brother to be contested. It is the foundation of the clan system of Saudi Arabia — the foundation of the royal family itself. The value of the company was estimated and Ali was given his share. He then left for Lebanon. Salem, and his younger brother Bakr, took over.

The company still had the prestigious and lucrative exclusive contract to renovate Mecca and Medina, but it was flagging elsewhere. Yeslam began to rise through the ranks. He hired two men from Citibank and began restructuring the main Jeddah office. Yeslam created departments, and implemented formal reporting and decision-making processes. He was the first to bring in computers, and little by little, he took over the company's finances, negotiating loans and investments with major foreign banking conglomerates. He began joint ventures with companies like General Motors, and Losinger, a Swiss construction company.

The Bin Laden Organization was jointly owned by Sheikh Mohamed's heirs, in a complex arrangement. The four wives who were still formally married to him when he died shared one-eighth of their inheritance among themselves. The remaining seven-eighths of the company went to his fifty-four children: a full share to the sons, half as much to the daughters. The company was operated in common — not even a parcel of land could be bought or sold without full agreement — and none of the brothers, at the time, received a salary. Every child took a dividend every year — one share for boys, half a share for girls.

Salem and Bakr had the same mother. Officially, there are no half-brothers in a Saudi family, but still there were affinities, groupings — whether because the men shared the same mother, or because they were the same age, or had gone to the same schools. If they had all three factors in common, as Salem and Bakr did, the tie was even closer. Yeslam's natural allies were all younger than him. And like many of the younger men, he chafed under his older brothers' rule.

One evening, when everything was closed, Yeslam took me to see the offices. I was carefully shrouded, of course, in my *abaya*. The building was near Kilometre Seven and it looked like — like nothing. It bore no resemblance to a major Western corporation, all glass and power. It had long corridors, like

133

an old provincial high school in Europe, with bare little rooms. Somebody was sweeping — just sweeping, not even using a vacuum cleaner — so I had to retreat into Yeslam's office. It was simple: a wooden table, no carpets, and just three cheaply framed pictures on the wall, of King Abdel Aziz, King Faisal and King Khaled. It looked nothing like the head office of one of the most important companies in the Middle East.

The other brothers soon realized that Yeslam's skills were vital. Yeslam's place was at the Jeddah headquarters of the business now. He was consulted. He knew about finance, and about the West. But some of his older brothers didn't welcome Yeslam's growing stature. His reputation was starting to overshadow their own. To maintain his position, Yeslam badly needed powerful allies. Hassan was a very capable older brother who had no natural confederates, since his mother had had only one son. Hassan became Yeslam's ally, even though Yeslam came just tenth in rank and Hassan was fifth.

The lines of allegiance were constantly shifting, according to unspoken disputes and private agendas. If Omar wanted to buy a piece of land, he might temporarily join with Yeslam's camp, say. Like any corporation, this one was rife with internal politics. But it was

134

also a family — and a carefully polished family, where no strife could ever be openly acknowledged.

The atmosphere of tension and secrecy was often stifling, and it began to weigh on Yeslam's spirit. He turned to me increasingly for support and reassurance, to cope with the pressure he was under from his brothers. He needed a sounding board. I had become his strength. I found I was becoming a strategic counsellor, an analyst, with a hoard of secret knowledge of the day-to-day goings on behind the scenes. It was a role I welcomed: it kept my mind functioning, and it helped me feel involved in building a future for our family.

Yeslam was by now in effect the Chief Financial Officer of the company. Many of the younger brothers began coming more often to our house in the evening, to drink tea on our terrace or have dinner and talk. I would stay to eat with them, and listen, and since Yeslam did not order me away they accepted my silent presence. Perhaps they did not realize that I knew enough Arabic to understand. The most religious among the brothers — Osama and others — rarely visited at such times, because I kept my face unveiled. If they did come, I had to retire to my room.

I learned to keep my own counsel. If I spoke, the brothers would go silent, and Yeslam would glare at me over his tea glass. I learned to stay still and absorb knowledge. Many issues were not clearly stated, but I could divine the intended message. Later I might talk with Yeslam about what I had learned.

Sitting on my terrace sipping tea, this coterie of younger brothers would discuss business: decisions they planned to make, or counter-orders that Salem and Bakr had issued. Many of them were frustrated by their lack of contact with the princes of the al-Saud family, who ruled the country with total power. Cultivating a benevolent, powerful prince could cost you much time, in lobbying, and also money. It involved paying court to them virtually every evening and travelling with them. Some of the al-Sauds skimmed a huge percentage off every major contract as their divine birthright, but the princes were also the gateways to success, prestige and clout.

I didn't want Yeslam to remain the tenth in rank, a clever cog in a machine that was much larger than he was. I knew that he was brilliant, effective and skilled — he deserved more than that. But to become his own man, more than just another Bin Laden, Yeslam would need his own contacts within the al-Sauds. Salem and Bakr guarded their contacts with the Princes closely. These were doors on which you could not simply knock.

As our social life expanded, thanks to our Thursday night parties, we were meeting many more people. My friend Ula Sabag's husband, Issa, was a soft-spoken older man who worked as a translator and counsellor at the American Embassy. He was well-placed in the entourage of Prince Majid, a portly, pasty-white figure who was one of the King's many brothers. Like all the major al-Saud princes, Prince Majid received people every evening at his *majlis*, in a vast, regal room in his palace. It was a kind of court of supplicants, after the evening prayer. If they were not well known to him personally, Prince Majid would simply greet the visitors, and they would take their place on some distant settee. Close associates would be seated beside the Prince. That was the nexus of power.

Well-connected people might attend several such courts, as Salem did. He had many close sponsors, among them Prince Salman, the governor of Riyadh, and attended a different *majlis* virtually every night. One evening, Issa took Yeslam to meet Prince Majid. Nothing special transpired that night — a little conversation, some cups of tea. Things happen slowly in Saudi Arabia, in symbolic steps so infinitessimal that an outsider might not even notice. But soon a pattern was set. Yeslam became close to Prince Majid, then to other Princes too. He was becoming one of the men who sat close to power. He was talking, now, to other men who sat close to power as well. It was a subtle play of influence and gestures that had enormous impact on Yeslam's stature.

Later on, when Issa Sabag retired, he came to see us. He had lost his own position with the Prince, but he had some administrative request, and asked Yeslam to take him along as part of his entourage. Yeslam agreed, but day after day he would avoid the old man before heading out to see the Prince. One day I cornered him and said, 'Issa helped you when you needed him.' But Yeslam dismissed me imperiously. 'Nobody helped me,' he said. 'I am a Bin Laden.'

But that was many years later. As Yeslam began consolidating his power within the Bin Laden Organization, the discussions on my terrace became more heated. Yeslam was now in effect running the company, and although they were earning big, new contracts, Yeslam's rise was not welcomed by Salem and Bakr. One morning Bakr called a major bank to discuss a loan for a new building project. The banker foolishly asked, 'Does Sheikh Yeslam know about this?' Bakr felt slighted. He had lost face.

Salem and Bakr began issuing counter-orders to Yeslam's decisions. They claimed credit for his projects and undercut and criticized his key employees. They turned down agreements he had negotiated at the last minute, embarrassing him. Then Hassan, who was a good businessman, but lost a lot of money at a London casino, phoned for help. Salem paid Hassan's debts, but when he returned to Saudi Arabia, Yeslam found him detached. Hassan had switched camps.

Yeslam organized a major new contract to build the Bin Laden Plaza in downtown Jeddah. It was a spectacular skyscraper, in those days by far the tallest building in town, which cost hundreds of millions of dollars to construct. We made a lot of trips to Paris during those months and it was Yeslam who negotiated the contract and signed the agreements. We spent weeks at the plush Georges V hotel; I remember sitting on the bed, cross-legged, reading the contracts late into the night.

For the Bin Laden Organization, it was a fantastic financial coup — the first in a series. The entire project was financed by French bank loans and guaranteed by the French government. All the company did was put up the land. When the entire building was rented to Saudia, the national airline, the French quickly recouped their investment. The Bin Laden Organization subsequently made a fortune as the owners of, essentially, a free building.

Of course this could never have happened in any other country, because the French would simply have bought the land. But in Saudi Arabia foreigners cannot own property, or even practise business without a Saudi partner. Again, the sacred soil cannot be sullied by unbelievers.

I was so proud of what Yeslam had achieved in setting up the project, but when it was reported in the Saudi papers they gave all the credit for Yeslam's work to smug Bakr. I could see that it gnawed at Yeslam, but he would always back off at such times. He never confronted Bakr and Salem with what they were doing, although his private dislike of them grew even more vehement. He complained to me about his brothers' tactics, but he never took action to defend himself.

Confrontation is not a Saudi habit. On the surface, everything is calm, particularly within the clan. There is greed. There are struggles for power and honour — even among the royal family. The hidden daily reality is brother against brother, for even in Saudi Arabia, human nature pushes individuals to affirm their personality and ambition. But in a deeper sense, their shared social conditioning and Wahhabi convictions mean that members of a Saudi clan will always support one another. No individual destiny is more important than those shared religious values. For a Saudi, there can be no escape from the traditions of his ancestors.

12

1979

On New Year's Day of 1979, I reflected that change had come to Saudi Arabia. My three years there had seen a gleaming new city rise out of the sandy dirt roads of medieval old Jeddah. Modern amenities were coming — no longer did the Bin Laden truck bring water to fill our cistern every two to three days. My girls were happy. I had Haifa for comfort and fun. Yeslam adored me, and his scope and power were growing. Some young women even risked walking in the malls with their faces uncovered. I had everything to look forward to.

How could I possibly know how many steps backward the Middle East would swiftly take? In the coming months, a rebellion against the Shah in Iran would trigger a shockwave across the region and give the traditionalists' fight against every attempt to bring the Middle East into the modern world new momentum. Islam would take on a completely new dimension and change the outlook of the entire world. Nothing would ever be the same again.

Not even the lapdog Saudi newspapers could shield us from the news that was flaring up in Iran. Revolution had broken out. In January, Shah Reza Pahlavi was forced to flee the country. A weird, awkward coalition of Western-influenced liberals and fanatical fundamentalists was calling for rule by the people. In February, Ayatollah Khomeini left his exile in France and arrived in Tehran, to be greeted by unbelievable crowds of millions of sympathizers. Then Khomeini's men began attacking the Westernized liberals who had helped them. They forced the veil on women who had previously chosen to walk the streets uncovered. Businesses were targeted for Islamic 'reform'. Everyone could feel the sudden, sinister wind of change.

At our Thursday evening parties, the diplomats and other foreigners could speak of nothing else. Everyone was insatiable for news. I was among the lucky ones: my sisters in Europe sent me newspapers and magazines weekly by DHL. I was overwhelmed by what was happening in Iran. My mother's home-land was being transformed by a revival of the Middle Ages. Acid was thrown in the faces of women who wore make-up. Thousands of people were arrested and killed. Khomeini criticized the Saudi monarchy, and said there could be no king in Islam.

I could see that the spectre of revolution made Yeslam and his brothers nervous. I, too, watched anxiously. If the monarchy could be overturned in Iran, if free Iranian women could so swiftly be forced back into the chador and suffer vicious attacks by the religious police on the street — then what could happen in Saudi Arabia? I worried, too, about the people I knew in Iran. My mother was safe, in Europe, though she seemed increasingly frail. Most of her family had already emigrated, many of them settling in America. Still, she had countless friends and acquaintances living in Iran, and news of their living conditions was difficult to obtain and horrendous to imagine.

Deep down I still thought that if ever there were a revolution in Saudi Arabia I would be able to escape. As a foreigner, and as a Bin Laden, I knew I would be among the first to get out. That was the true luxury in my position, not the Chanel dresses and emerald earrings. We had the clout to get out if we had to — the power and status to escape the inspections of the religious police, get out of jail, or get out of the country. The Bin Laden Organization had a fleet of commercial aeroplanes, and if a Bin Laden wanted a seat on a plane, he could just take one. As the Bin Laden Organization was the only company authorized to work in Mecca, the family's status was far higher than that of the other merchant clans. Even if an aeroplane was fully booked, Bin Ladens would always get a ticket. I had often seen this happen. In case of trouble, we could surely just fly ourselves out.

So, although I was tense I didn't feel directly threatened. But the al-Saud princes who ran the country must have been much more frightened than I was. They had everything to lose. Khomeini's revolution was an outright attack on their rule. You could see the increasing influence of hardline religious ideas on the street. The tiny changes that had given me so much hope for future freedom crumbled as the royal family panicked and sought to placate the fundamentalists.

More extreme ideas of religious behaviour took grip with a swiftness that stunned me. Notices were plastered in the souk warning about the dangers of improper dress. As sermons in the mosques began calling for greater restrictions on social mores, more and more women began wearing the veil again. Despite the punishing heat, they added thick black stockings under their *abayas*, to shield the few centimetres of feet and ankles that might be seen as they walked. Many, like

Osama's wife Najwah, and my sisters-in-law Rafah and Sheikha, started wearing gloves. As in Iran, the *mutawa* began wielding thick long sticks, to police our modesty, sometimes beating women in the street.

One afternoon, I was in a supermarket when a pregnant woman fainted and her husband rushed to help her up. The *mutawa* stopped him, yelling at him that he must not take his wife in his arms in public. If the prayer call rang out when we were shopping, we couldn't stay, as before, while the men went out to pray: the shopkeepers were frightened and closed their shutters hurriedly. The *mutawa* would yell at us in the street, 'You, woman, what are you doing?' if our hands were showing, or if my *abaya* was held too high. Abdou, my driver, would always protect me saying 'Bin Laden.' Even now, the religious integrity of a Bin Laden woman could not be questioned. Nonetheless, I began to be afraid.

The *mutawa* broke into homes and smashed hi-fis. If they found alcohol, they hauled men off to jail and beat them there. They prohibited the sale of children's dolls, which became contraband, like whisky, because they were human images. Suddenly, the only dolls for sale were shapeless figures with no faces, like the one owned by Aïsha, the Prophet's child-wife, in the seventh century. But this was 1979!

There was no discussing such matters with the Bin Laden women. They would never have violated the rules in the first place. To them, the *mutawa* were doing their job, and that job was honourable and just. They felt certain there was no such thing as being too strictly religious, but the foreigners all noticed how much more severe and terrifying the *mutawa* had become.

Once I did strike up a conversation on the subject with Rafah. We were talking about the veil, and I told her I found it unnecessary and insulting — insulting to Saudi men. Were they really so weak and so obsessed with sex that they would be tempted to sin by a mere glance at a woman's face? Rafah stared at me as though I'd been speaking ancient Greek. I could read it in her eyes — 'poor ignorant foreigner.' I simply could not get through to her.

It was the young people who frightened me the most. They were supposed to lead the country forward. I watched them week by week as they sped backwards through the centuries. I saw their gloves and black stockings and their angry faces, heard the demands for more restrictions. Surely it could not be true that they were in fact longing for the world to move into reverse? Who could believe such a thing? And yet it was happening in Iran.

I felt trapped. Every one of the changes I had welcomed seemed to have been temporary. Every little opening lasted so briefly. The Saudis had opened up to the world for a couple of years. Now, it seemed, they were stepping back to their values and traditions.

We went to the United States that summer. It was partly a business trip for Yeslam, but mostly I wanted to fold myself into Mary Martha's reassuring, loving embrace. She was delighted to see me after the months of terrible upheaval. I felt such relief to be back in America again, but the day before we were scheduled to leave Los Angeles for St Louis, where Yeslam had meetings, Mary Martha phoned me, in tears. Her brother Jimmy had been lost flying his own plane between Arizona and California. A search was out and she was flying to Arizona to be with her parents.

I couldn't leave Mary Martha at a time like that and insisted that we stay with her. Yeslam went into overdrive. By the time Mary Martha and I reached Arizona, he had chartered two planes and was co-piloting one of them in the search for Jimmy. A whole fleet of planes stayed up in the air, dawn to dusk, till the wreckage of Jimmy's plane was found, five days later. Yeslam's face was tense and drawn. He didn't want to talk. I remembered that his own father had been killed in a plane crash, when Yeslam was only seventeen.

My heart went out to Mary Martha and her family, but we had to go back for Yeslam's business. We returned to Saudi Arabia, hearts heavy, words unspoken. It had been a dreadful summer.

All of Saudi Arabia seemed mesmerized by the political volcano in Iran, and its fallout across the Middle East. It was all we talked about. One of our occasional guests, John Limbert, an American diplomat, played tennis with us one Thursday night in October, and told us he would be leaving for Iran the next day. Then, a few days later, he was taken hostage in the US embassy in Tehran. He and dozens of others were paraded before the TV cameras to demonstrate the might of Islamic vengeance on the godless Americans. John was among the group of fifty-two hostages who were held in captivity for 444 days. Lois West tried to comfort his wife Parvanai through her terrible ordeal; we were all shaken.

Then one November morning Yeslam rushed home from work, ashen and agitated, and told me, 'Mecca has been taken.'

Hundreds of Islamic extremists had stormed the Grand Mosque and seized control of Islam's holiest place. Through the muezzin, their leader was making incendiary statements about the corruption and loose living of some of the al-Sauds, particularly Prince Nayef, the governor of Mecca. The extremist forces had sneaked into Mecca using Bin Laden Organization trucks, which were never searched.

We must have been the first to know. The Bin Ladens had permanent staff in a maintenance office in Mecca. When the rebels stormed the Grand Mosque, a Bin Laden worker immediately phoned the head office in Jeddah and reported that violence had broken out. Then the insurgents cut the phone lines. Incredibly, it was the Bin Laden Organization that informed King Khaled that rebellion had broken out in Islam's holiest city. One of his first decisions was to cut all phone lines. I wanted to phone my mother, to reassure her, but there was no way to get a line out. The newspapers didn't dare report the attack for several days, but information spread anyway. There was tumult everywhere and air traffic was grounded.

The house filled, then emptied, in a frenzy of movement as brothers rushed in and out with the latest news. Yeslam was frantic, dashing from house to office like a man unhinged. The Bin Ladens had the only detailed maps of Mecca — the Grand Mosque in particular and Salem stayed with the princes day and night. After days of discussion and attempts to negotiate with the extremists, they laid out plan after plan for military assaults on the extremist-held Mosque. All of them failed.

Then Yeslam told me his brother Mahrouz had been arrested on the road driving from Mecca to Jeddah. The police had found a pistol in his car. Mahrouz was a very strictly religious man now, though he'd spent a few years in Lebanon enjoying a Western lifestyle. He wore his *tobe* short to show his ankles and demonstrate his strict simplicity. Otherwise, though, I'd thought of him as just another of Yeslam's brothers.

Finally, the famous French GIGN para-troopers were called in. They flooded the Mosque basement with water, killing many of the extremists. (They had to undergo the world's most rapid conversion to Islam before they could approach the building.) In a country with no journalism, rumours ran wild: the French had electrocuted the rebels; it hadn't been the French at all; the rebels hadn't really been captured. Then dozens of men were executed in public, across the country.

Then Mahrouz was freed from jail. Had Mahrouz really been involved in a plot against the al-Sauds? I knew there were many rumours that he might have been involved, but nevertheless he was released. People said he was the only suspect to have been freed from police custody.

In early December, we heard that violence had erupted in Qatif, in eastern Saudi Arabia. There had been riots and many deaths. This was a region inhabited by a small minority of widely reviled non-Wahhabi Muslims — they were Shi'ites, like most Iranians. Perhaps influenced by Khomeini's revolution in Iran, the Shi'ites had taken to the streets in unusual numbers that year for their annual procession to commemorate the death of the Prophet Muhammad's grandson, Hussein. The *mutawa* had intervened in the procession. The number of deaths was unknown, but an open rebellion had lasted several days. Yeslam's panic grew more hysterical, and though I tried to calm him, I, too, was frightened. What would become of us all?

Then, barely three weeks after the Mecca revolt, the Soviet Union invaded Afghanistan.

World events seemed to be closing in on us. Already unhinged by a neighbouring revolution and a spectacular internal revolt, and enmeshed in growing radicalism in their own country, the Saudis now watched Soviet tanks rumbling through another nearby nation. The aggressive, atheist Communist monolith had attacked a country of poor and deserving Muslims. The al-Saud princes were stunned, like everyone in the Muslim world. After weeks of inaction, the princes decided they must demonstrate that they did indeed care about fellow Muslims. They would fund the Afghan resistance.

Yeslam told me that announcements were being made in mosques to encourage ordinary people to give cash, equipment and used clothes to the Afghans who were fighting the Soviet soldiers, and to the refugees who had begun to flee. The government announced it would give huge financial support to volunteers who went to Afghanistan to support the brave mujahidin, their brother Muslims. Among the volunteers was my brother-in-law, Osama.

Osama had just graduated from his studies when he took up the cause of the Afghans. He left quite quickly — there were no farewell parties. With his great stature and his strong opinions, Osama was an arresting figure, but he didn't seem like the best choice for a leadership position in the Afghan resistance. Nonetheless, he started to make frequent long trips to Pakistan, helping with the logistics of funnelling Saudi aid to the volunteers. He helped set up clinics and training bases in Pakistan, and soon he more or less lived there year-round, becoming increasingly involved in the Afghan struggle.

Then Osama started moving into Afghanistan itself. According to his sisters, who spoke of him with awe, he was becoming a key figure in the struggle. He imported heavy machinery and manned earth-moving equipment to blast out tunnels through Afghanistan, to house field hospitals for the fighters and stocks of weaponry. He built dugouts to shield advancing Afghan warriors as they attacked Soviet bases. We heard that he had even taken up arms in man-to-man combat.

Osama was making a name for himself. He was not just the sixteenth or seventeenth Bin Laden brother any longer. He was admired because he was involved in a noble cause. Osama was a warrior — a Saudi hero. Along with almost everyone else in Saudi Arabia, Yeslam and I made donations to the Afghan struggle. We packed up all the clothes we didn't need, and sent money.

Osama was not the only family member whose attachment to Islam was becoming more demonstrative. Some of my sisters-in-law whom I had always considered tedious and submissive surprised me now with their activism when it came to defending Islamic values. Sheikha, one of Yeslam's older sisters, even went to Afghanistan herself to distribute an enormous consignment of aid to the needy. She went with a retinue, of course, and saw no fighting, but I had to hand it to her, she wasn't just murmuring the Koran and defining correct behaviour — she was brave enough to take action.

In Afghanistan, as in all wars, women were shouldering the worst of the burden. Afghanistan was like a nightmare come true for a mother: all those young women and children fleeing into camps, sitting destitute in the rain, herded like animals by rough-voiced men. It was terrible. Even worse was to come, when years later the Taliban fundamentalists took over.

1979 was a turning point for the whole Islamic world. For me it was as if a harsh spotlight had been focused on my own life. More sharply than ever, I realized that I was living in a fragile bubble, surrounded by a foreign culture that was subject to sudden outbursts and explosive violence. I was still so young, only in my mid-twenties, and we'd been married for just five years. Yet I had so many responsibilities and worries. I had to protect my children. My mother's health had deteriorated; news of the situation in Iran seemed to have destabilized her emotionally. She refused my invitations to visit Jeddah and I felt unable to leave Saudi Arabia.

Meanwhile, Yeslam remained agitated and fearful. He began having nightmares, waking me up at night to play backgammon to calm his nerves. I sought to reassure him. As the world beyond our walls seemed sometimes to be crashing around us, I watched my husband turning into a fretful, childish stranger.

13

Yeslam

I realized that something was really wrong with Yeslam. It was not just some passing mood. He was nervous all the time and he had nightmares. He was frightened of everything, especially dying. He had various physical complaints — belly aches, trouble breathing, sudden sweats of panic — that required endless tests, but which never seemed to amount to anything precise.

Not since the Mecca revolt had Yeslam really been happy, I thought to myself. At first I'd thought that the political situation in Saudi Arabia was the cause. First the shock of 1979, and then the unpredictable backlash, as Saudi Arabia began to swing sharply away from the path I'd thought the country would choose. Money had changed Saudi Arabia enormously, but those sudden changes only touched the surface. Money bought many things, but they were only things; they brought with them no shift inside people's minds. The new buildings, the bigger houses, the huge modern shops and European vacations — these things didn't seem to be leading to freedom. Money was tugging Saudi Arabia towards the modern world, but the dour, puritanical, self-assured culture was tugging the country back to its extreme, traditional restrictions.

Perhaps there was a similar struggle going on inside Yeslam, too. He was under increasing stress. When Salem and some of the other brothers had begun manipulating the Bin Laden Organization against Yeslam, I encouraged him to stand up for himself. A meeker woman — a Saudi woman — would have told him, 'Ma'alesh, that's life,' and encouraged him to stay in the position God had allotted to him, the tenth son. Yeslam could have submitted to the rule of his less competent older brothers, and taken refuge in his religion and tradition. But I was not that kind of woman. I couldn't allow that to happen. I didn't want to see him give in and submit.

I'm a fighter and I encouraged Yeslam to fight. I urged him to confront his brothers, and to change things. I told him that he was the brightest and the best of them. I needed him to help change the Saudi way of thinking — for my sake, and for the girls'. I couldn't change anything myself, because in this

158

society there was no way I, as a woman and a foreigner, could achieve anything.

Only Yeslam, with his intelligence and his power, could give me hope that the country might yet make those crucial shifts which would bring us more freedom. Perhaps a Saudi wife would have given Yeslam more peace of mind, but I couldn't accept his weakness — and to be honest, I was panicking too. I pushed Yeslam to strike out on his own, so, in 1980, he simply stopped going to the office. He set up a brokerage in Jeddah, and a big financial company in Switzerland, hiring a highly skilled staff to make investments for the newly rich Saudi merchants. It was a success — that became clear quite quickly. Yeslam's companies were going to do very well. I felt smug about that, and I told him, 'You'll see. Salem and Bakr will be begging you to come back.' They did and offered Yeslam a salary to return to the Bin Laden Organization. It was the first time a family member would be paid over and above the annual dividend.

By this time, Yeslam was beginning to be worth a truly enormous amount of money. At the time I met him, Yeslam's share of the Bin Laden Organization was probably worth no more than fifteen million dollars. Most of it was tied up in the business, and it never seemed real to me. Now, however, with the company flourishing and his own businesses taking off, Yeslam's personal worth rose to something closer to three hundred million dollars. He was one of the wealthiest of the brothers — as rich as Salem and Bakr. In practical terms, it didn't make much of a difference to our lives. We continued to fly commercial. I never bought vast amounts of haute couture, but I knew we were becoming extremely wealthy — I felt it was something Yeslam could be proud of.

But Yeslam was not happy, despite his obvious and soaring success. He was working more, spending long mornings at the Bin Laden headquarters and then going to his own office after the evening prayer, working sometimes until 9 p.m. or 10 p.m. Among the brothers, the rivalry and petty squabbling continued, as did the nasty blows below the belt that ate away at Yeslam, undermining his ego. On the surface, his relationship with his family remained courteous, but I knew that things were tense with his brothers. Once Yeslam said to me, 'Salah used to be over here all the time. Now, when Bakr washes his hands, Salah is there holding out the towel.' The cabals were out, whispering against him.

By striking out for himself and rising above his rank, Yeslam had committed an almost unpardonable infraction of the unwritten social code. It was not just I who had pushed Yeslam to break away from the social conventions. He was ambitious for himself, too. He responded to my encouragement because it was the direction in which he, too, wanted to grow. Yeslam had lived in the West and seen a culture that allowed you to make something of yourself on your own. But to do that, you must think and behave as a Westerner. And Yeslam was a Saudi.

If he had been encouraged more as a child, I'm convinced Yeslam's talents could have really emerged, but his mother was a fatalist. 'It is the will of God,' was one of her favourite phrases. I tried to give him the encouragement I thought he needed, but the contradictions of his culture nagged at him. So although part of Yeslam longed to achieve his own, individual ambitions — as a Western man would — another part of him needed to remain submissive, to occupy the space allotted to him in his tradition-bound culture. Yeslam was split between two utterly irreconcilable impulses. I see that now, but then, I only saw his ailments, and a new weakness and distance in my husband.

Yeslam constantly consulted all sorts of medical specialists abroad, as Saudi doctors made him nervous. I thought a psychiatrist might help him sort out the problems that I felt were more psychological than physical, but Yeslam refused to see one. Then I managed to find a Western doctor in Jeddah with whom he felt at ease. Matthias Kalina was in charge of the military hospital. He and his wife Sabine became great friends of ours, indeed, years later, when they had moved to Canada, Yeslam used to fly Dr Kalina to Switzerland to discuss his health. Dr Kalina prescribed Temesta to calm his nervous tension. But Yeslam used to cut each pill into tiny fragments and swallow just one piece, which of course had no effect.

He became frightened of flying alone, so I accompanied him everywhere, scheduling trips for the girls' school vacations so they could come along too. (I never left them alone in Saudi Arabia, not even for a weekend.) He couldn't stand crowds. One summer we went to Los Angeles and stayed in Ibrahim's house for six weeks, and, except for the usual visits to doctors, we must have left the house only three times.

Yeslam was becoming a stranger to me. I cared for him so deeply, and relied on him so much, that I tried not to look too directly at the reality of his condition. I needed him to remain the clever, emancipated man whom I had married. I longed for the warm, attentive father, and the thoughtful, caring husband I once knew. I simply could not deal with the reality of this petulant, frightened stranger. I had to persuade myself these were simply moods — something temporary. I don't think anyone apart from me could see that something was wrong. Yeslam was adept at maintaining a perfectly unruffled exterior, but, in reality, he was having a kind of nervous breakdown.

This led to a very personal milestone of my own. It was the summer of 1981 when I realized that I was pregnant again. We were having a family vacation in Geneva, and at first I felt so happy. It may not have been rational given my track record, but I was convinced that, at last, we would have a son! I rushed to Yeslam with my glad news, expecting him to be as happy as I was, but he had a strange look on his face that I had never seen before. He said he had always wanted just two children. He told me that he was only just beginning to recover from his illnesses and he couldn't cope with another child. He asked me to have an abortion.

I felt numb. My joy gave way to turmoil. Why would he not want another child — perhaps a boy? But I wanted to help Yeslam. I believed you shouldn't force a man to become a father if that's not what he wants. Yeslam's reaction was so strong and he seemed so adamant, that I worried he would always resent the child if I went ahead with the pregnancy. Perhaps especially if the child should be another girl. As much as I wanted this child, I agreed to have an abortion.

We returned to Saudi Arabia. I thought I could put it behind me, but I had dug a moral hole for myself that I would never be able to climb out of entirely. Although I could shut off my waking brain, I couldn't close down my dreams. I began having nightmares. Always, Wafah and Najia were taken from me. I had destroyed a child, and now I no longer deserved to be a mother. Life was dark then. I felt I had done something terrible.

I was angry with myself that I didn't have the strength of mind to stand up to my husband. I had done everything for Yeslam, but now I felt that he had asked me for something unbearable — something he should never have asked me to do. He had behaved with unbelievable selfishness. And then, when it was clear that I was suffering horribly from this awful decision that he had demanded I make, Yeslam acted as though nothing important had happened — as if I had had a tooth extracted. But I knew that what I had done was immeasurably more awful. I had abandoned my unborn child, and my husband had abandoned us all.

We went through a bad patch after that. I felt very low. With hindsight, I realize I was depressed. Although I tried to knit a normal life together for the children, there wasn't much joy in it. I felt alone then, in an aching, new way. Deep down I had always thought that I could count on Yeslam, but now, though I had always been there when he needed me, he did not, or could not, give me the same support. I couldn't understand Yeslam, and I felt he failed even to try to understand me. Perhaps this was the beginning of the end.

14

Little Girls

Even in my darkest days, I tried as best I could to bring up my daughters to be free — to grow up as themselves. Behind the high walls around our house, I thought I could build a small space where we could try to live normal lives, where I could attempt to reconcile the differences between my values and those of the world outside. I bought them bicycles and roller-skates, and taught them to swim in Haifa's pool. The girls both loved music; they were constantly rehearsing and putting on little shows for Yeslam and me. All through their childhood, my funny little girls were always play-acting, dressing up and miming songs by my idol, Elvis.

But dancing lessons were an impossibility in Saudi Arabia. Music lessons were too, although my girls were fascinated by classical music. One afternoon when she was just three, Wafah listened spellbound to an entire Tchaikovsky piano concerto that she'd asked me to put on. 'Put on the 'Big music', Mum, *la grande musique.*' A friend of mine was visiting me that afternoon. I remember how struck she was to catch sight of Wafah, motionless and intent, almost wrapped around the loudspeaker. She had real potential, I think — something special. But the simple, normal development of my daughters' artistic talents was out of my reach in Saudi Arabia.

I tried my best to give them the kind of childhood I wanted for them. I invited foreign families with boys of their age to visit us. Sometimes they even spent the night. I wanted Wafah and little Najia to see boys as just people, like they were — the way their little cousins never could.

I was demanding with them, as well. I knew they were materially privileged so I was determined that, from an early age, they should understand the value of work in order to appreciate the work of others. This was very important to me.

Yeslam and I seized every opportunity we could to go to Switzerland, where we'd bought a manor in a small village outside Geneva. There I lived as I wished, wore what I wanted to. I could drive myself to a movie, I could walk the streets alone. I taught the children to ski and bought books like a mad woman, sighing as I thought of the long, dreary months in Jeddah.

I always dreaded returning to Saudi Arabia. For the children, too, the transition between our two worlds was sometimes brutal. When they were small, they would always try to tug the *abaya* off my face when I cloaked myself as we circled above Jeddah. Then, as they grew up, they stopped trying. I didn't know which was worse. I realized with a start one spring afternoon in 1981 that now the time was swiftly approaching when my little girls would have to go to school.

To this day, there is no legal obligation to educate girls in Saudi Arabia. Many Saudi men do not send their daughters to school, and very few of them feel it is important. Even boys' education is relatively recent. Until World War II, there were only traditional schools teaching Arabic, a little Islamic history and the Koran. Then, in the early 1960s, Princess Iffat, the wife of King Faisal, faced down tremendous opposition from Islamic leaders and set up Saudi Arabia's first girls' school, Dar el Hanan. This was where Yeslam proposed we send Wafah, aged six, and little four-year-old Najia.

I knew it would be hard for them, but I had no choice. Saudi children were not allowed to go to the foreigners' schools. Moreover, my girls were Bin Ladens. I could not isolate them from their father's culture. They had to face this challenge, and for the first time, they would be alone. I had shielded the children from much of Saudi Arabian culture, and as a result they didn't even speak proper Arabic. I tried to prepare them, told them they would make friends and learn Arabic, and that it would be lovely. I watched them enter their classes in their dark-green pinafores and frilly white blouses, my heart sinking. They didn't cry.

Saudi children are trained very young to adhere to a strict social code. The certainty of a woman's inferior status and subservience is bred into their bones as they grow. In the car, Haifa's older son — who was only ten or twelve — would instruct her sharply to veil if he saw men coming. Little girls knew they must walk, dress and talk unobtrusively. They had to be submissive, docile and obedient. It was common to see a young boy walk into a room and motion his older sister off her chair.

At school, what those children met was a form of brain-washing. I watched it happen to my daughters. Lessons — Arabic, maths, history — were learned by rote, parrot-fashion, with no deeper understanding of their real content. There were no sports, no debates and no discussions. No games, marbles or tricycles. Religious education was the most important class of all, and it seemed to take up half or more of every day.

When Wafah was seven or eight, I looked through her exercise book one evening and I found she'd written down, 'I hate Jews. I love Palestine,' in her childish Arabic script. What was happening to my daughter? If she was going to hate somebody, I wanted her to have a good reason. The Arab-Israeli dispute was something she knew nothing about.

The next day I went to the school principal and said, 'My daughter doesn't know where Palestine is. She knows nothing about Israel. She isn't even doing geography yet. How can she be taught to hate what she doesn't know about?' The principal, a small but imperious woman, was completely impervious to my protest.

'This is not a matter for you to discuss,' she told me. 'You are a foreigner, you cannot understand. Does your husband know about this?' I tried to remain dignified. I said my husband was completely aware of my position, and that I would ask him to phone her. Then I went home, called Yeslam, and had him phone the school and tell the principal that I was in full charge of the children's education.

It was a kind of victory — I wanted her to

know that Yeslam gave me full authority over the children, something few other Saudi wives could claim. But I knew deep down that I could do nothing to prevent the school from trying to teach my girls to hate blindly along with reading and writing. I had no choice. I must merely hand them over from 8 a.m. to 2 p.m. every day. I just had to accept this, and it became one of a long list of things I began accepting against my will.

Still, although I could not change their schoolwork, I was their mother and I could influence my children. I began a conscious effort to teach the girls how to reason, how to deduce things and how to think for themselves. I would pick them up from school and over lunch we would often discuss the news or religious tolerance. I laid out a programme for after-school activities — structured play with Playmobil and plasticine, and sports. The girls would learn music. Perhaps, I mused, I should hire a tutor to come to the house.

I didn't care that Wafah got high marks in school. I knew that her teacher would always give a Bin Laden the best marks, whether she deserved it or not. Everything was glossed over in that way. And, in any case, her grades only reflected Wafah's quick memory, not her understanding of her lessons.

One day, exasperated, I met with her classroom teacher and told her I wanted her to treat Wafah the same as the others. A few days later, Wafah came home sobbing. Her teacher had hit her across the face. I went back to the teacher, not to make a big protest, but to say simply that I thought this was not the best method of discipline. Irate, the woman said Wafah was a liar, that she had never done such a thing. She asked the children, 'Wafah is lying, isn't she? I didn't hit her, did I?' But one brave child, another half-foreigner, raised her hand and said Wafah had told the truth. That poor little girl had a miserable time for the rest of the school year.

I quickly understood that my intervention in school was doing no good, but I couldn't watch my children become educated in this way. Though I hated to load the girls down with extra work, I hired a female teacher to tutor them after school, and told her I wanted my children to understand, not memorize, their lessons. The teacher never asked me what I meant — a Saudi woman does not say she doesn't understand, because it would mean losing face, but I could see she was struggling to figure it out. And I think in the end she realized it was a better way to learn. It certainly saved my little Wafah and Najia's brains.

On another occasion, Wafah came home crying again. There had been music in school and she had begun dancing. A schoolmate hissed at her to stop. 'It's *haram*,' she told Wafah. 'Dancing is *haram*. Don't you know anything?' What do you do when your child asks you if dancing is a sin? 'Dancing is not *haram*,' I soothed her, 'You can dance.'

I could have warned her to dance only at home, in private, that these things might get her into trouble one day. But how can you tell your children that music and dancing are sinful? These countless, endless, foolish, mean little restrictions chafed at me. I couldn't force them on my daughters. The words of Kahlil Gibran haunted me as I brought up my little girls.

Your children are not your children.

They are the sons and daughters of the desire for Life itself.

They come through you but not from you, and though they are with you, yet they belong not to you.

You may give them your love but not your thoughts, for they have their own thoughts.

You may house their bodies, but not their souls; for their souls dwell in the house of tomorrow, which you cannot visit,

173

not even in your dreams.

You may strive to be like them, but seek not to make them like you.

For life goes not backward nor tarries with yesterday.

I treasured my children. I tried to give them my love, acknowledging that they had their own thoughts. Though around me I saw a completely different kind of upbringing, a different vision of respect. You would never see a child contradict his father. For me, respect goes deeper than that — Mary Martha's example had taught me this. I think that the more you love someone, the more you should be able to say difficult things — superficial agreement is for strangers. I wanted my children to know more than me, to be cleverer than me, to disagree with me and show it.

I respected my children's characters and opinions, just as much as I wanted them to respect mine. Respect to me had become something that I should try to earn by my actions. I didn't want my children to feel they were obliged to accept all my ideas. I didn't want them to be cowed. I wanted them to say no to me, because if they could do that they could say no to the world — and grow up to become the people they wanted to be.

But at school, my girls learned the fear of hellfire. They began to worry about my soul.

'If you don't pray, Mummy, you'll go to hell,' Najia would say, staring up at me with her big, innocent eyes. It hurt me horribly, every time, to see the worry in her eyes. I would say my faith was a matter between God and me. That the most important thing was to behave in a way that helped others, and did not harm them. I told my little girls I didn't want them to pray because they were frightened of hell. Prayer is not something you do for bargaining with God, I would explain, it is an intimate request to reach inner peace.

It was a topic that I broached from time to time with some of my sisters-in-law. Ultimately, it was pointless, however, as their certitude was absolute, but with my children, the lesson sank in — perhaps too well. Despite their young age they were able to form their own opinions. One day the King decreed that all the nannies in Saudi Arabia would have to become Muslim. Our Filipina maid, Dita, told Wafah and Najia that she was ashamed that the King said her religion was not correct. Wafah asked her if she believed in Islam, and then drew herself up in shock when Dita said she didn't.

'Why would you change if you still believe

in your religion?' she asked Dita. 'What will your mummy and daddy think of you? My mummy will never make you change your religion, you know.'

I thought it was cute, but also rather deep and clear-sighted of my little daughter, and that Friday when we lunched with my mother-in-law I told her the story. Om Yeslam's reaction was unexpected. Frowning, she told me, 'You have closed her door to paradise.' Wafah, at seven, had realized that Dita's belief was the issue, not the appearance of believing. But my mother-in-law was convinced that pretending to be a Muslim was infinitely preferable to being a believing Catholic.

I began to fear that by bringing the children up with Western ideas I was doing them no favours. Slowly, imperceptibly, it seemed we were developing two different mindsets, along with our two different wardrobes for Switzerland and for Saudi Arabia. In Geneva the children wore little T-shirts and frilly short shorts, and I wore a bikini at the seaside in Cannes. They went horse-riding and learned to water-ski. Yeslam permitted it all because they were young — it didn't matter. And they were abroad, so it somehow didn't count.

My children were beginning to enter a

world that was not mine. The first time I saw one of their cousins wearing a veil I yelped, 'Already?' The abstract idea that my children were growing up was becoming more real. Soon it would be Wafah's turn to cloak herself in darkness. There was a little leeway: very religious families would veil their girls at nine, but others waited until puberty, at twelve or thirteen. But every girl had to veil in public once she had her first period. I dreaded the day, though I tried to reason with myself. After all, *I* wore the *abaya*. It was not the end of the world, merely a foolish inconvenience.

Watching as Saudi society seemed to drift deeper into rigid fanaticism, I could no longer be confident that one day my daughters would be permitted to choose *not* to wear the veil if they wished. I looked at my own *abaya*, trimmed with faint silver embroidery: it seemed, suddenly, a hideous garment, ghastly in its blackness and terrifying in all it represented. I realized that by bringing my children up to believe in freedom, tolerance and equality, I was shaping them into women who would rebel from a society seeking to lock them in. And as Princess Mish'al's murder had amply demonstrated, a rebellious woman may be marked for death.

I was a foreigner, but my husband was gentle and understanding. No other Bin Laden — none of the Saudi men I knew — could have tolerated my Western values. Would Wafah and Najia have as easy a life as I did? Or would their husbands be more like the dour, reserved Bakr? Like Mahrouz, the formerly Westernized brother now turned Islamic hard-line extremist? Or, appalling thought, like rigidly puritanical Osama? Saudi men were so unpredictable: an apparent liberal could shift position in a few months, become devout, and impose strict Islamic mores on his wife.

I had chosen my husband. I received men in my home, and had dinner parties. Would my children be able to make the same choices? Or would they marry a cousin, perhaps, in a family arrangement, and be delivered to him, mind and body, come what may, for the rest of their lives?

My daughters' marriages could break down; my own marriage might fail one day. That idea takes on even bigger proportions in Saudi Arabia, where your husband holds the key to the only tiny freedoms a woman can hope for. I had seen too many women deprived of their children, their independence, their minds. But if my girls were not submissive, what lives would they have?

It gnawed at me. I had been free to choose, and I had chosen a life that was restricted in many small ways, along with some big ones. By making that choice, however, I had ensured that my daughters would not be free to choose as I had chosen. In my nightmares I saw my little girls growing up to become Saudi women — bent over under the weight of their subservience, cloaked in darkness. In those long evenings, as I faced the dusk outside my terrace, I no longer even saw the black birds flying across the empty desert. Now it was my worries that wheeled around my head, nagging at me.

15

A Saudi Couple

As Yeslam grew stranger, I also came to feel increasingly distant from the Bin Laden family. I lived for the school vacations, counting the days till we could head for Europe or the United States, and my own version of freedom. Still, when Fawzia, Yeslam's younger sister, became engaged, it was inevitable that her giving-away ceremony would be conducted at our house in Jeddah. Just as Yeslam was my legal guardian, he was her head of the family too.

Of all the women in the Bin Laden family, I was most familiar with Fawzia. She was Yeslam's only full sister, Om Yeslam's only daughter, and we had lived in the same house for over a year. She had always lived with her mother, and, until she was married, the two of them even shared a bedroom. Fawzia had a mighty view of her own importance. She was pretty — she considered herself the prettiest of the Bin Laden sisters. As a full sister, she always felt that she should have greater importance in her brothers' lives than their wives did.

I should have been close to Fawzia, but I couldn't be — I felt that she envied my special relationship with her brother. She realized I wasn't blind to the wiles she used to obtain concessions from her future husband or even her brothers. For me, relationships are straightforward. If I wanted something from Yeslam, I would ask him directly. When my mother encountered financial difficulties, I simply asked Yeslam to help her, which he did. I was outspoken about the things I felt really mattered, and Yeslam and I could openly debate them.

Fawzia had been brought up to avoid that kind of clear, direct behaviour. Like many other Saudi women, she had learned how to manipulate men in a subtler, more oblique manner to obtain what she needed. If they wanted to go overseas, they would always come up with a plausible excuse, like a medical appointment. If they needed more money to buy something, they'd invent some household bill as a pretext, then use the money for their own devices.

Once, I had to buy presents for friends overseas, and Yeslam gave me two hundred thousand riyals (about fifty thousand dollars) to go to the gold souk. I went with one of my sisters-in-law, and when we got back I showed Yeslam what we'd chosen, adding 'There's sixty thousand riyals left over.' I put the money on the side table. My sister-in-law was surprised. She chided me, 'Your husband gave you that money. You should keep it for yourself!' But Yeslam and I never lived that way. There was almost always a box of cash in the house — two hundred thousand riyals, or sometimes ten times that much — that I could use as I wanted. Why should I do something underhand?

Sometimes I would be talking with my sisters-in-law and realize they had absolutely no knowledge of what I was talking about, but they would never own up to it. (Later I might overhear them repeating it to someone else, though.) Saudi women never openly admire something that belongs to someone else, either. They denigrate people, their looks, their way of dressing and their household, but then they copy them constantly — even as they express their scorn.

Fawzia and I came from two different worlds. Perhaps her background and her place in that male-dominated society meant that she simply had to learn to be manipulative in order to get what she needed. I admit I can be vain. I, too, like luxury — the things that money can buy. In those days I had five or six fur coats for my trips to Europe, a safe full of jewellery, and a walk-in wardrobe filled with *prêt à porter* dresses. I never asked the price of anything — if something attracted me, I bought it. But for so many Saudi women, shopping was like a compulsion — a frenzy to fill the emptiness and boredom of their lives. They didn't seem to buy things because they appealed to them. They bought them because other women had them, and they wanted more, and better, things than everyone else. Once, Yeslam gave me an emerald necklace. Fawzia sniffed at it, then went straight out and bought one too.

Still, when Fawzia was getting married, I was happy for her. She and Om Yeslam seemed so thrilled. We were in Geneva when we heard that arrangements had been finalized for her engagement to Majid al Suleiman, who came from one of the important Saudi families. She told me she needed a dress, and I rushed out and bought her a beautiful one from Givenchy. It was pink and white, with silk ribbons, the bridal dress from the latest haute couture collection. Fawzia turned her nose up at the dress — it was too simple — but when she saw that the sisters-in-law loved it, she wore it anyway. I don't remember her thanking me, though. She was so sure of her own superiority. It always came down to the same thing — she was a Saudi, and I wasn't.

For Fawzia's *melka*, the engagement party, we pulled out all the stops. We strung the garden with thousands of lights, and laid out plans to serve hundreds of women. But then, the night before the wedding, Fawzia threatened to call it off. She wanted a marriage contract that would ensure she could initiate a divorce. I had never heard of such a thing. In Saudi Arabia, divorce is simple if you're a man. He merely recites 'I divorce you,' three times in the presence of witnesses and the thing is done. A woman, however, must struggle through the complicated procedures of a religious court, and her only hope for divorce is on the grounds of manifestly un-Islamic behaviour. (Adultery and beatings don't count.)

The *melka* was postponed for two days. The florists took back the enormous flower displays, and everything went on hold. Then Fawzia got her contract and the party went ahead. As the guests arrived and threw off their *abayas*, it was like a competition for who could wear the heaviest make-up, the most jewellery or the most expensive haute couture dress. Fawzia and Majid arrived separately, to the ululating calls of the women. They were seated under a canopy where they signed the register. This was the part of my own wedding that I had missed — it was the register I had signed in the car because Regaih's *melka* had happened before I arrived in Saudi Arabia to be married. Fawzia's actual wedding party took place weeks later, in a hotel. For now, though, Fawzia and Majid were legally engaged and finally had the right to spend time together without a chaperone.

Yeslam and I liked Majid. He was twenty-two, rather younger than his wife, handsome, with classic features and a beautiful smile. He was a very sweet-tempered man, much more tolerant of others than Fawzia was. Majid was witty and he had a great sense of humour. We talked and laughed together. In the summer, when we went to Geneva, we went about in a foursome. Once, he saw me wearing a silver fox coat, with a natural grey sheen. Majid, who loved being playful, exclaimed, 'What, you gave the poor animal grey hair?' He looked over at Yeslam, and said, 'Careful, man, don't stay too close to your wife, you'll be getting grey hair too!'

Wafah and Najia adored Majid. He was such a kind and patient man. Once Fawzia, Majid and I were getting ready to leave their house to go somewhere. Majid and I were waiting downstairs, and he visibly winced as he heard Fawzia reprimanding the maid, who had burned a hole in the carpet while ironing on the floor. 'Why not just buy the poor woman an ironing board?' I thought to myself.

Fawzia had two little children, Sarah, and Faisal. Like so many wealthy Saudi children, little Sarah was indulged in material ways, but she never really had much sustained adult attention. She had boxes of toys she didn't know how to play with, and almost no discipline. One day, I watched as little Sarah tore up packs and packs of playing cards. Fawzia never tried to teach her respect for objects or people. If she got tetchy, Fawzia would just wave her over to the maid who was just a household servant. The poor woman looked after Sarah and Faisal from morning to night, in addition to doing the household chores. If a child cried, it was the maid's fault, but there was never a word of gratitude for her work. Dita, our Filipina maid, used to help my children fall asleep by lying down next to them on the bed. This simple domestic ritual became a problem if the girls ever napped at Fawzia's house, as Fawzia's maid was not permitted to use the furniture. She wasn't even allowed to sit on a chair while feeding the children.

Majid was a moderating influence on his

wife, but one day, tragedy struck. Majid had a passion for cars and he bought himself a Formula One racing car. It was bright green, and known to all. It raced under the colours of the Saudi airline, and was the pride and joy of every teenage boy in the country. The day the car was delivered, Majid decided to drive it. But the car's acceleration was far too powerful, and driving out of the garage it jerked forwards. Majid's head was thrown backwards against the roll-over bar, and he was knocked unconscious.

They took him to the university hospital, where he revived. A doctor sewed up the wound at the back of his head, but he was haemorrhaging internally, and he soon lost consciousness again. Neurosurgeons were flown in from London, but it was too late. Majid's brain stopped functioning, and his body followed a month later. He was wrapped in a simple shroud and buried at sunset, in an unmarked grave, in the desert, as the Wahhabis do. No women were permitted to be present.

I was completely devastated, and I could think of nothing else. Majid, so sweet-natured and funny, was only twenty-seven. How could he be dead? I prepared for the three-day mourning period at his mother's house, when all the women in her family would be present, to keep company with Om Majid and Fawzia in their grief. (Yeslam went with the men, to Majid's father's side.) When I got there I found a room full of women wailing loudly, dressed all in black or in white, and Fawzia in full make-up on the sofa. She had recently given birth to Faisal, who was just two or three months old, and when Om Yeslam asked if she needed anything, Fawzia said 'A girdle.'

I was dumbstruck. To be worried about your appearance at a time like this! I expressed my sympathy for her loss. 'It's God's will,' she said. 'Maybe it's all for the best. Perhaps if he had lived he would have divorced me and taken my children.'

Again, appalled, I tried to focus on the children. Faisal was crying. He hadn't been bathed, so I took him and washed him, and then I took little Sarah out to a merry-go-round to distract her. I spent the three-day mourning period as silently as possible. One of Majid's sisters was distraught, and I told Fawzia I was worried about her. 'Oh, her,' Fawzia said. 'During our five years of marriage, we hardly ever saw her. She's being melodramatic.' It was as if Fawzia didn't want anyone else to feel what she manifestly wasn't feeling.

A few days later, we got the news that one

of Om Yeslam's brothers had died in Iran. Fawzia was all over Om Yeslam. 'Oh, mama, poor mama.' I couldn't stop myself from asking, 'Fawzia, how long has it been that Om Yeslam has not seen her brother?' She threw me a sharp look, and I think after that she really did hate me.

A few days later, before leaving for Geneva, I decided to express my regrets one last time to Om Majid. She was a gentle woman, and I liked her. Fawzia asked my driver to carry over a note. When the note was handed over to Om Majid, I saw her wave to her houseboy. 'Give the driver the money,' she said, her face still worn by grief. It took me a few moments to realize that Fawzia had sent her mother-in-law the two thousand riyal bill for her cook's salary. I wanted the ground to open up.

16

Sisters in Islam

Fawzia never showed any evidence of compassion in her soul, but she prayed five times a day, as did all the Bin Laden women. The most orthodox of them was Sheikha, who was close in both blood and spirit to Osama, though far more meek, of course. The younger Bin Laden women all admired her, even the mothers-in-law looked up to Sheikha because of her religious devotion, particularly after she began working for Osama.

I visited Sheikha often, as I did many of my sisters-in-law. I needed to understand the culture my children lived in, and my husband's roots. Sheikha and her husband had built a house nearby, but we were never close. Saudi women don't open their lives to each other as American or European women do — and especially not to a foreigner.

Still, I would visit. It was an activity. Sheikha would ask me for news of Yeslam, and I would enquire politely about the health of her family — even this simple dialogue was ritualized, a minefield of hideous possible errors. Sheika could use my husband's name in conversation as she was his sister, but I could not say her husband's name, even though she was my sister-in-law. To speak his name out loud, or ask about his health would presume a form of intimacy. That was a place you could never go. I had lived so long in Saudi Arabia that I no longer noticed these stiff, polite rituals of segregation.

Despite everything, I was fond of Sheikha. She had energy and vigour, though it all went into pursuing her religious beliefs. Sheikh Mohamed's eldest daughter, Aïsha, also had quite an energetic and commanding appeal. She was very close to Om Yeslam — they had breastfed each other's children. All the Bin Laden women seemed to accord Aïsha a special place, as befit the eldest of the great Sheikh's daughters. She was also older than many of his wives.

Aïsha was short, but very dignified, and also relatively outspoken. When I arrived at her house, she would often complain that Yeslam didn't come by to see her more often. It was bold — no other sister would ever complain about a brother. But the implied criticism never went too far. Once I arrived at some family gathering with Yeslam, and spotted Aïsha in the room. 'Look, you don't have to tell me about Yeslam not coming to see you any more,' I said to her. 'He's here! You can tell him yourself!' The whole group was aghast. I had invited Aïsha to take my husband — her brother — to task, in public! The silence that followed my remark seemed endless.

The only break in the protocol that ruled relationships among the Bin Laden women was a small, but perceptible, jealousy of one of the sisters, Randa. Randa was an only child, and although she had no full brothers, nevertheless she was privileged because she was Salem's favourite, and he was the eldest brother. Salem never refused Randa anything, or so the women said. It was almost scandalous, they muttered, the way Salem took her everywhere, travelling with her even outside the country — sometimes, even without his wife. In fact, they whispered, if Salem travelled abroad with Randa and took his wife along, Randa would sit beside him in the car while his wife was relegated to the back seat.

I would have thought that in a world of women, there would be companionship and spontaneity, a warm, supportive understanding. But among the Bin Laden women every gesture was always very proper, highly ritualized, and almost completely static. My friend Haifa, Bakr's Syrian wife, had a more natural understanding of the proper codes of conduct than I did, and she had to help me learn them. I was a good social mimic and eventually I did manage to perform the correct conversational rituals at the endless afternoon gatherings I felt obliged to attend. But they frustrated me. Nothing ever seemed to go deeper. It was such a large family, with such an enormous amount of to-ing and fro-ing, but the contact between them seemed so superficial.

Then, one afternoon, Sheikha invited me to attend one of her religious study meetings. The chosen sisters filed into her living room and listened quietly while a woman scholar droned on, reading and interpreting the Koran. You could tell who the fervent ones were by their gloves, thick and black in the Jeddah heat. Many wore head-scarves now all the time, even though only women were present.

The force of their religious conviction gave some of these women a leadership role — Aïsha, Sheikha and Rafah, another, rather pretty, older sister. I think that Rafah was genuinely concerned about my immortal soul, while I wanted her to open up a little to the wider world. We often debated the merits of Saudi Islam's restrictions. She was always preaching the correct Islamic behaviour. The younger women, like Osama's retiring young wife Najwah, would always voicelessly agree.

I did genuinely like some of those women. Om Yeslam was kind and gentle. I enjoyed Sheikha's energy. Rafah's mother, like Sheikha's, was sweet and welcoming, and Taiba, who had lost her children when her husband divorced her, was mild and warm. I think they liked me, too.

Still, attending that religious study meeting in Sheikha's house that afternoon, I realized how deeply in the minority Haifa and I had become. I watched the women seated around me, and listened to them talk as if they were in a movie. I felt like a complete outsider. Najwah was particularly unsettling, perhaps because she was so meek. She was constantly pregnant, and by the time I left Saudi Arabia for good, she and Osama had had seven sons and she was not yet thirty. With drab clothes and downcast eyes, Najwah seemed almost completely invisible.

What could I talk about with women like this? What can you say to someone with whom you have nothing in common? There I was, thinking to myself, 'What does this girl have in her life? She is pious . . . religion is her entire world. She cannot listen to music . . . she bears children and her husband doesn't let her out.' She might smile at me, probably thinking to herself, 'Poor woman, she will go to hell,' and I was thinking, 'Poor woman, she is *living* in hell.' We had totally opposing convictions.

It seems to me that Islam, more than any other religion, bites deeply into the everyday life of a believer. It is not just a theology, it is a vastly detailed way of life. To a strictly orthodox Muslim — and the Saudis are of the strictest kind — no separation of religion and state is conceivable. Islam is about Islamic law: the code of behaviour and law is as fundamental to religious practice as the Koran. The shariah — the body of Islamic law — is the constitution of Saudi Arabia. There is simply no possibility that the government, or Saudi society, could ever be divorced from the strict rules of Wahhabi Islam.

Sheikh Mohamed bin Abdul Wahab, who reinvigorated Saudi Islam in the 1700s with his extreme puritan revivalism, was convinced that the Islam he saw around him needed to be purified, to be taken back to its seventh century roots. Sheikh Wahab insisted that no interpretation of the Prophet's law could be permitted. Islam was to be taken whole. It could not be modernized or reassembled. As a result, the Saudis have become the guardians of absolute orthodoxy in the Islamic world. The only difference between Saudi Islam and that of the ultra-hardline Afghan Taliban is the opulence and private self-indulgence of the al-Sauds. The Saudis are the Taliban, in luxury.

Living in a modern, global economy means that the Saudis have had to change in at least some ways, and to adapt their society, no matter how slightly. But even simple innovations like automobiles, photographic images or television, require rulings from Islamic scholars to determine whether or not they are permissible under Islam — partly to pacify the people who are angered by such modern changes, and partly out of simple conviction. The Saudis fund movements to export their strict Wahhabi form of Islam to the outside world. This became a particularly intense concern after the Soviet invasion of Afghanistan.

When I was living in Saudi Arabia, it was always said that six per cent of oil revenue went to propagate Islam around the world. In addition to that official spending, great families sponsor evangelist Islamic movements, so mosques in Europe, Asia, and America are built and funded by Saudi Arabia. Their preachers adopt the hard-line message of Sheikh Wahab, to Muslim cultures

196

which have evolved to become more tolerant and more flexible.

Scholars are brought to Riyadh and Jeddah to be educated, and return to their homelands to spread the word. The Saudis pressure the people who receive their financial aid to enforce strict rules — to ban alcohol, impose fasting during Ramadan and minimize the education of women and their access to the workforce. Saudi Arabian Islam is an enormous, very wealthy power that seeks to change the world, and it stretches far outside the borders of that otherwise firmly closed country.

As the years went by, I came to see how incredibly defensive Saudi society is about other religions, even the country's flag boldly announces 'There Is No God But Allah.' No religion other than Islam may be practised in the country. No Bibles may be brought in, no collective prayer is permitted. Many foreign workers, such as my maid, Dita, suffer great pain from this ruling.

In other ways, too, Saudi Arabia exerts an almost paranoid control over the millions of foreigners it must import to design and operate the machinery of modern life. Except for diplomats, every foreigner who enters the Kingdom must be sponsored by a Saudi, who takes his passport for 'safekeeping', and who exerts enormous control over his actions. No foreigner can even leave the country without the permission of his sponsor: getting an exit visa requires the sponsor's signature. They may not own property in the country, and in order to go into business they must have a Saudi partner.

Women who marry Saudis often find themselves trapped in the country if their husband, or ex-husband, will not permit them, or their children, to leave. Without his signature, there can be no exit visa; without an exit visa, there is simply no route out.

Living in Saudi Arabia I always felt somehow clandestine, as though I had snuck into the country under false pretences and could never show my true nature. When I looked at women like Najwah, Rafah or Sheikha, I was afraid for my daughters. These women did not chafe at the restrictions they lived under, they embraced them. Even after many years in the country, I could only hazily understand that terrible, self-enslaving mindset.

At the time, I thought my children's destiny lay in Saudi Arabia. I loved my husband, we lived in his country and my girls were Saudi. I knew that I should teach them the codes of behaviour that would ease their lives there as adults. They must learn — and learn as young as possible — to operate as Saudi women. Their well-being and peace of mind might depend on this, as well as countless small freedoms that required male permission. Still, try as I might, I never could manage to teach my daughters to practise the manipulative behaviour that characterized the women around me. Perhaps, for their good, I should have made that effort, but I felt powerless to prepare them for lives as Saudi women. I hated even thinking about it.

When I could bring myself to reflect on Wafah's and Najia's future, I realized that I was raising my children to become rebels in Saudi society. I knew they might suffer for that, but I was also afraid, deep down, that my girls would become like Najwah and the others, that they would adopt the way of strict religion and leave me. I didn't want my children to become black-gloved, mute strangers, that I could not have borne. I would not have wanted my sweet, gay little girls to grow up that way.

Najwah was a submissive person by nature, I think, and her upbringing had made her fatalistic. She never permitted herself to want more from her life than obedience to her husband and father. It would drive me crazy. I would think, 'God gave you arms and legs and a head, to think with, so use them.' I found myself becoming frustrated, as a woman, to be surrounded by women who simply did not have the courage to resist the system.

Sheikha and Rafah did have courage, only they threw it all into religion. I think that was simpler for them than fighting for their rights as human beings. Piety gave them the illusion that they had power. I think they believed that if they were very strictly religious, then the men, like the other women, would respect that, and it seemed to work. I'm sure their fierce piety was a matter of personal conviction, but it was also partly a necessary tactic for them, I think. When you live as a complete dependent, you have to learn how to influence your master: there may be no other way you can survive.

Another way a Saudi woman can hope to influence the men who control her is to manipulate her children, particularly the boys. Women were always more indulgent with their sons, and I noticed that when a husband was around, they would be even more attentive. If you were a fine mother then your husband would never divorce you — that was the theory. And a son would one day be your legal guardian in your husband's place. A husband might stray, or die, or divorce you, but a devoted son would always stand by his mother.

I didn't have sons, and the other Bin Laden women — even Om Yeslam — didn't seem to care much about my daughters' upbringing. I would do the dutiful daughter-in-law act, and prattle on. There was no other subject for neutral discussion in those long, tedious afternoon teaparties. I would report that Wafah and Najia had learned to pray, that I had taken them to Mecca, that they had learned Arabic and could recite this or that section of the Koran. But Om Yeslam never enquired about such issues. I couldn't help thinking that she cared far more for Fawzia's little girl Sarah.

I was trying to make her love my children, but I don't think I ever succeeded. Perhaps it was because I was a foreigner. One day, much later on, when Yeslam and I had moved into a larger house in Jeddah, Wafah was playing with a little half-English schoolfriend, running around the house screaming and wet from the pool.

'Ah, that foreign girl,' snapped Om Yeslam, exasperated.

I answered her back rather tersely, 'We are all foreigners to somebody.'

'Not me,' Om Yeslam answered, looking straight at me. 'There is not one drop of Christian blood in me.'

I did have a drop of Christian blood in me — my father's. And so did the girls. But what Om Yeslam really meant was that I had a determined, wilful personality, and she felt that I would simply never bring myself to submit in the proper manner to Islam, to the rules of Saudi society, or to my husband — and she was right.

17

Princes and Princesses

I first met my dear friend Latifa in Geneva, at a lunch one day with Fawzia and Majid. Yeslam and Latifa's husband, Turki, enjoyed each other's company. We became friendly, the four of us, and Latifa and I became close. Latifa was an al-Saud, a princess. I had met Saudi princesses before, and I hadn't been particularly impressed. The few I'd met had been trite and unbearably superior, but Latifa was not that kind of person. She was interested in other people, and she didn't have the arrogance of some of the other Saudi royals.

Latifa was tall and had a languid poise. She was one of the most beautiful women I had ever met. She was very different from me — very quiet. I used to joke, 'Latifa, the walls are tired of hearing only my voice.' She was so reserved that we never spoke much about her family or political events. But Latifa liked having an outsider around, someone who had no part in the shifting mass of courtiers within the royal family intrigues, and I liked her because I saw in her a true Arabian princess. It wasn't just because of her striking beauty, but because something inside Latifa was noble in a very deep sense.

Latifa's husband was a member of the al-Saud royal family too, but he was shy and rather formal. In the beginning, even after he became friendly with Yeslam, he found it hard to be alone in a room with me. The first time Turki came to our house and found that Yeslam hadn't yet arrived I had to practically force him to wait inside. He sat bolt upright on the living-room sofa, not daring to look me in the face. It was one thing to see me unveiled in Geneva, it was quite another to be alone with me in a room in Jeddah.

Turki loved being in the West. He loved the relaxation of restrictions and the freedom to be yourself and socialize naturally with women as well as men, but in Saudi Arabia he snapped back to custom. Now that I'd lived in Saudi Arabia for so long, I could see that it was hard for Turki, too, to resolve the contradictions of living in two worlds. He was one of the few Saudi men I truly liked. Later, when I left Saudi Arabia for good, he gave me his support. I will always be grateful to him for that. Latifa, too, has been loyal. She is the only Saudi woman who has stood by me to this day.

Latifa and Turki lived in the compound of one of several mansions his father had built for his children. These were not palaces; although Latifa and Turki were royals, they were not from a major branch of the al-Saud family that might one day inherit the throne. Yeslam told me he probably had more money than they did.

Latifa's father, Prince Mansur, was a respected older relative of King Khaled's. When he travelled, he would request the use of the King's own aeroplane — one of several which contained a fully equipped operating room on board and countless servants. It was not easy to say no to Prince Mansur. He was a strict man, and he was accustomed to demanding complete obedience from his daughter. When Latifa was eight years old, her father divorced her mother who was then banished. Latifa didn't see her again until after she married Turki, who permitted his new wife to contact her mother.

Even as an adult, Latifa would obey her father's directives unquestioningly. Once, he felt that Latifa had been in Europe for too long. At the time, he was visiting one of his properties in Spain — it wasn't that he wanted to see her — but he demanded that

Latifa return to Jeddah right away. Even though her husband was in Europe with her, Latifa went back to Jeddah at her father's command. She was gentle, and clear-sighted, but obedience had been bred into every cell in her body.

Latifa was a wonderful person, but she was also a good Saudi woman. If she'd lived in Europe, Latifa could have made use of her intelligence, she could have been strong and free. She could have developed her personality so much further, but, brought up in Saudi Arabia, her character was weakened, stifled into submission. She was very fatalistic. If something went wrong, she would say 'There's no point thinking about it, it's done.' There was no revolt left in Latifa. She'd learned to stop asking questions. I think her spirit had been broken. Latifa had known Princess Mish'al, the young girl who was killed by her grandfather for falling in love. That was one of the issues that she never wanted to think about.

Like every other Saudi prince and princess, Latifa and Turki supported their lifestyle almost wholly out of the stipend which they received from the Treasury every year. Even small children receive this income, and it is calculated by age, rank, power, and gender. Girls receive half the share of boys. In

206

addition, all public utilities are free for princes, and many of the most powerful princes (though not Latifa or Turki) trade their influence with every layer of the Saudi government for huge percentages of 'commission' which are skimmed off all major business contracts.

This is the Saudi system — an accumulation of more and more people into a royal family that treats the country's oil wealth as its personal treasury. Abdel Aziz ibn Saud, the first King, who created Saudi Arabia out of the desert, had at least seventeen wives. When he died in 1953, he left behind forty-four sons. I don't think anyone knows how many daughters he had, even the number of his wives is a matter of speculation. Before he died, Abdel Aziz laid out the succession. Saud, the eldest son, would follow Abdel Aziz as King, and would be assisted by the second eldest son, Faisal.

King Saud was a disaster. He was a spendthrift, self-indulgent and petty where Abdel Aziz had been austere and cunning. By 1958, dissatisfaction with Saud's rule led a group of important princes and religious leaders to step in. Faisal, the Crown Prince, ruled the country in Saud's name for two years, but he tried to limit the royal family's spending, and Saud regained control in 1960.

After a few more years of Saud's rule, the country was veering on the edge of financial disaster. So, in 1964, the religious leadership issued a ruling that Saud was unfit to govern the country. Faisal was named King, and Saud went into exile, living in Europe till he died in 1969.

King Faisal was a moderate, dignified man, and his rule is generally seen as having improved the country immensely. He sought to limit the princes' abuse of their positions. Then in March 1975 King Faisal was shot by one of his nephews, an Islamic radical.

The next heir would have been Prince Mohamed, a violent and fiercely conservative man who would later order his young granddaughter, Princess Mish'al, to be put to death. It is said that the royal family feared that war or rebellion would quickly break out if Prince Mohamed took the throne, and he was persuaded to step aside from the succession. Khaled, the fourth son of Abdel Aziz, became King.

King Khaled was rather mild, paternal and popular. His reign coincided with Saudi Arabia's boom years. When he died of a heart attack in 1982, he was succeeded by Crown Prince Fahd. Fahd was not the next son in line, but the royal family seemed to have concluded that he would be the most suitable candidate. Much weakened by multiple health problems, King Fahd remains on the throne to this day and is likely to be succeeded by his brother Abdallah, who is now over seventy. But nothing is definite, the succession is not a clearly stated law, but the result of consultations in secret councils of the royal family and religious leadership. It is said that King Fahd, or his clan, opposes Abdallah, who is deeply conservative, and has criticized the loose morals and high living of his family. The infighting is said to be intense. It is a strange kind of non-system, and the uncertainty of the succession keeps an enormous crowd of courtiers buzzing with power struggles and rumours.

Naturally, the Bin Laden clan is prominent among those courtiers today. Salem died in a flying accident in Texas in 1988, and his rule over the family has passed to Bakr. Bakr is allied to King Fahd's favourite son, Abdel Aziz. To Yeslam's irritation, Bakr is now privileged among the privileged at court.

Sometime in 1994, just before our divorce procedure began, Yeslam confided in me that King Fahd's health was deteriorating. He said that Prince Abdallah was likely to take over. He added that many conservative princes were supportive of Osama, who had been forced to leave Saudi Arabia after he publicly condemned the loose living of some of the Saudi princes.

Osama had gone into exile in Sudan, Yeslam told me. He had a group of armed followers, and tanks that guarded his compound. Yeslam believed that when Abdallah took over the throne Osama's star would rise and Bakr's power would fade.

That was before Osama's name was linked to a series of terrorist attacks on Saudi Arabia and the West. I know nothing of Crown Prince Abdallah's view of Osama Bin Laden today. But I know that to this day, no Saudi prince or member of the Bin Laden family has acknowledged that Osama directed the attacks on the Twin Towers.

To date, the King of Saudi Arabia has always been one after another of the ageing sons of Abdel Aziz. None of his grandsons has yet taken over the throne, which may be one reason why Saudi Arabia never changes. The family keeps growing. Latifa told me there was always at least one al-Saud child born every month, so there are great and great-great-grandchildren now. By the time I lived in Saudi Arabia, there were more than five thousand princes in the royal family. Some say the al-Sauds now number over twenty-five thousand members.

When Abdel Aziz ibn Saud named himself

King in 1932, Saudi Arabia was desperately poor. His first palace was made of the same sun-dried mud bricks that the peasants used. In those days, Sheikhs and Bedouin herdsmen called each other by their first names. Then oil was discovered in the 1930s. Since this was Abdel Aziz's country and it was even named after him, it was, I suppose, considered natural that the oil wealth should go principally to his children. They lived in unbelievable extravagance. Oil was their personal harvest.

The princely practice of skimming percentages was not considered immoral by any Saudi I ever met. Yet at the same time, it was *haram* to gain interest from a savings account, because the Koran forbids the practice of usury. I couldn't understand contradictions like this, even if I did sometimes find them amusing. Once Yeslam's brother Tareg owed a bank a considerable sum of money. He refused to pay the interest, claiming it would be un-Islamic, and as far as I know nobody ever made him do it.

However, many princes were not in the high spheres of power and their stipend didn't even approach the millions of dollars of annual income reserved for the King's brothers and sons. Often, to supplement that income, they would open their own businesses, as the commoners did: small contracting, fashion boutiques and interior design companies. Decorators were flying into Jeddah by the dozen in those days. Everyone was redoing their houses, in a kind of frenzy, because everyone else was, but not quite knowing how. There was a fierce kind of competition going on. Huge luxury mansions, the most glamorous that money could buy, would be topped six months later by even greater, grander versions. There was marble everywhere in these homes, halls as big as a hotel lobby and gaudy chandeliers. It was like walking into a furniture store with no harmony, everything over-sized and ill-matched.

Latifa and I would meet, talk and lend each other videos. We went out shopping together. On one such trip, she was amused when she and Yeslam urged me to buy a beautifully embroidered haute couture dress at Chanel, in Paris, and I said I just couldn't bear to spend sixty thousand dollars on something which, in Saudi Arabia, I could only wear once. We cried together at *Sophie's Choice*. We talked about our husbands, and often, I would still be sitting in her living room when her relatives came to visit, as the afternoon drew to an end.

Some of the Saudi princesses whom I met then, and later, lived lives of such decadence and inertia that it was hard not to feel disgust. Although the princesses lacked for nothing in terms of material possessions, they also had nothing to do. As the queens of France did in the olden days, the princesses lived in separate houses alongside those of their husbands. Their houses were smaller, with a separate women's gate. They might share a kitchen or share one set of kitchen staff for the two houses, but otherwise they had two separate armies of servants — only women servants on the women's side. Their drivers were male, but they were always accompanied if they went out — they were never alone with them.

The princesses would get up sometime in the mid-afternoon, get dressed, make phone calls, and perhaps play with their children. Then they could go shopping. By this time, there were expensive, women-only shops, with female Lebanese or Egyptian shop assistants, and you could actually see the clothes you were choosing without a black veil over your eyes. Inside their own homes they were free to wear miniskirts, plunging necklines and makeup, and they were free to do more or less what they liked, but they were still prisoners.

By the early 1980s there were a few restaurants in Saudi Arabia. One or two had initiated 'family' sections, where a man and wife could sit with their children — the wife trying to eat while fully veiled, attempting to expose not one inch of skin. Some restaurants also had women's sections, where you could take your veil off, and the waiter would knock before entering: you quickly veiled for every change of plate or fresh bottle of Perrier. So there was this activity for them, too: a strange, sad little version of a restaurant.

At dusk, the princesses would visit each other or prepare for dinner — a women only dinner. Often you could hear the dinner going on in the adjoining husband's house. The wife might even phone her husband to advise him to serve this or that delicacy. Conversation was mostly about clothes or gossip. The food was never very good, but it was abundant: great stews with beans and rice, and ornate baskets of fruit that tasted of nothing.

Many of the princesses lived on pills — prescription, naturally. They made a beeline for the chic doctors in Harley Street every time they went to London, checking into clinics for countless tests. Some owned gym rooms and had their own indoor swimming pools, but nobody ever swam that

I could see. They had bone density problems from the lack of sunlight and exercise, and heart problems from eating too much. I think a very large proportion of these women were depressed. They had no responsibility, and no control over anything. They lived in complete dependence, in a kind of waking slumber. It was no kind of life. If I had had no other aspirations for the future of my daughters perhaps I could have accepted that life for them, and we would be among them still.

There is such emotional emptiness in Saudi Arabia. People need human contact. They need love and approval, and a sense of shared thoughts. But these women, so cut off from the world, seemed to have no real links with their husbands, segregated since birth, they could not establish any kind of true contact with the opposite sex. Perhaps, as a result, some of the princesses had affairs with each other. They would fall passionately in love, become jealous and stage enormous sulks. I often asked myself whether these relationships didn't have their roots in the harsh sexual segregation that seemed to make it impossible for men and women to relate naturally together.

We had all heard rumours of a lesbian party circuit in Riyadh, where women would socialize and pick each other up. I knew of one Egyptian woman married to a high-ranking Saudi who fell in love with a princess. She was miserable when the princess left her. Probably in Riyadh they had rumours of such a circuit in Jeddah. I never actually saw these parties myself, but I was propositioned once. It was all too strange for me.

Most of the men probably didn't know their wives were sleeping with other women, and those who did may not have cared enough to want to stop them. Women don't matter to a Saudi man. Possessing them matters — matters crucially. Once they're locked in and breeding, what happens inside them doesn't count for much.

Homosexuality is forbidden in Saudi Arabia and punishable by public flogging. But many men have homosexual relationships, especially when they're young and still single. If two men hold hands in the street, as they often do, it's not seen as sexual. But if a man and a woman do it, even if they are married, it's perceived as obscene. People are shocked, and the *mutawa* surge up with batons. The habit of teenage homosexuality doesn't always go away, and in that respect the al-Saud princes are like everyone else — except perhaps more so. You hear rumours. A European decorator I once met told me he thought there were more gay men in Saudi Arabia than in Europe.

One Saudi man we knew well — and whose wife we knew well, too — once turned up at our house in Switzerland with a very gay German man sitting beside him in his blue Porsche. I didn't know what, if anything, they did together. I wouldn't have minded. People should do as they wish. But I knew this same man would never have turned up at our house with a woman who was not his wife. The hypocrisy of that way of living really got to me.

I didn't meet many of the al-Saud princes. I know that these women did have their male equivalents who lived lives of waste, ignorance and debauchery. You hear about them often enough in the West. I heard the rumours of planeloads of call-girls flying in for the weekend from Paris. I'm not sure these rumours are true — you would have a lot of trouble getting visas and authorizations at the airport for a crew like that, unless you were very highly placed. If such parties did happen in Jeddah, then Yeslam never told me about them.

But I did hear about such antics when princes were hospitalized in Geneva, in detox clinics, for heroin or alcohol, or cocaine. And, like everyone, I heard about the obscenely lavish sex parties in Europe.

In the summer, when the al-Saud court dispersed throughout Europe, Yeslam would often meet with Prince Majid, and later Prince Meshal, in Geneva. When he brought them home, I would retire upstairs. Once, I was walking through Geneva, shopping, in a knee-length dress, when I caught sight of Yeslam and Prince Meshal on the other side of the road. Yeslam crossed over to talk to me, but Prince Majid stayed where he was, and looked away slightly. Even in Switzerland, you don't look at another Saudi man's wife.

When I was abroad, I was free. I certainly wanted nothing to do with the al-Sauds when I was in Europe. I suppose Yeslam probably would have liked me to pay court to the wives and retinues of the Princes, who often rented whole floors of the best hotels in town. I gave them as little attention as possible, but occasionally I felt obliged to pay a visit. It was like being transported back to Jeddah. Sometimes one entire floor of a hotel would be transformed into a Saudi women's quarter. Stepping out of the lift, you would find the Jeddah servants, the pungent Jeddah incense, and the Jeddah patterns of behaviour.

Once, at a dinner party at the Saudi embassy in Geneva, I was seated beside the daughter of one of the princes, a flashy, overbearing woman. She launched into a story about King Faisal, who supposedly told her he had seen one man cause another to levitate into the air. I turned and said — not in an insulting tone — 'I don't believe you.' She was so outraged to be challenged that she swivelled in her chair and didn't address another word to me all evening. Like so many Saudi royals, she couldn't tolerate contradiction — especially from a foreigner.

I had no desire to be at the beck and call of these women, accompanying them on their shopping trips, dressed in the *abaya*. Wherever they went, they transported the Kingdom with them, and I didn't want to be there. Switzerland was where I could be myself. For those blessed few weeks, I clung to my own life. I wanted nothing more to do with Saudi Arabia.

18

Leaving Saudi Arabia

Yeslam's personal business was still flourishing, as was the Bin Laden Organization. Everyone in Saudi Arabia seemed to be making money, with building projects on a Pharaonic scale springing out of the sand almost daily. For three years, Yeslam had the only brokerage in Saudi Arabia, and the great merchant families, as well as many Bin Laden brothers, took their money to him for investment. (At the time, most of the Saudi Princes didn't invest with Yeslam as they didn't want another Saudi to know how much they were really worth.)

But Yeslam continued to complain of his ailments. He was tetchy and selfish. My husband was becoming more childish and demanding, more centred on himself and his more or less imaginary ailments. He refused to believe the doctors who maintained that he was in perfect health and was becoming increasingly detached from his family.

In the beginning, I'd always seen Yeslam's

Saudi nationality as a minor detail, but now he was slowly becoming more deeply Saudi. He was imposing Saudi culture on us. The girls were growing, and Yeslam was becoming more critical of their behaviour, and he seemed to want them to be more Saudi in the way they dressed. He snapped at them for wearing tight clothes or short shorts, insisting that they change before we went out — even in Geneva. He had always left me in sole charge of the girls, but now, I felt that he no longer trusted my judgement. It seemed like the well-being of our daughters didn't bother him.

As Yeslam was becoming more Saudi, Saudi Arabia was becoming more schizophrenic. The more debauched princes continued indulging in their privately lavish lifestyles, while at the same time the royal family enforced increasing restrictions on the ordinary people they ruled. Extremist ideas were taking hold everywhere. Some of the Bin Laden sisters began complaining that their children were being exposed to too much Western influence. The most narrow-minded sisters-in-law came up with a solution: they would set up their own girls' school in Jeddah, with much stricter Islamic instruction. They invited me to register Wafah and Najia there. Many of the other sisters-in-law registered their children.

221

Once, I would have scoffed at the idea, or attempted a passionate discussion with my sisters-in-law to explain why I thought they were wrong. Now, I merely smiled and murmured that my children were happy where they were. I could no longer bear to stick my neck out. I felt that it was useless. My hopes for real change were by now completely shattered. Nobody, not even Yeslam, would have understood, now, how horrifying I found the idea of sending my little girls to an even more restrictive school.

Only a handful of the cousins attended my children's birthday party that year. I suppose my sisters-in-law could no longer tolerate the music and dancing. In their view, my girls were approaching puberty, and they should be behaving more like future Saudi women than foolish Western little girls.

Yeslam and I had fallen into a routine of spending all of the children's vacations in our house in Switzerland. It became our real home, for good, in 1985. That summer the power struggles intensified and Yeslam complained endlessly of ailments as usual — his lungs were weak, his heart was not strong and his stomach pained him. When September came around, and it was time to return to Jeddah for the start of the school term, I found Yeslam still hadn't made any plane reservations. He said he felt too unwell.

The days crept past. I was only too relieved to scratch a few extra days of summer freedom, but by the end of September the girls were restive. I told Yeslam that they had to attend school somewhere. If he hadn't made plane reservations by mid-October, I would have to register them at school in Geneva.

I held my breath. By 15 October Yeslam still hadn't taken any action, so I drove to an International school outside Geneva. It was like a dream — computer labs, language labs, sports facilities and art classes. The school was mixed, and most of the children were from families who worked at the United Nations, and they were bright and joyful. I spoke with the principal, explained the situation, and registered Wafah and Najia for the semester. Then I went home, and told Yeslam that I had made temporary arrangements for the girls to attend school.

Their first day, they wore jeans, like everyone else. They came home bursting with information. There were boys in the classroom! There were no classes in religion, no more hours of learning the Koran by heart. There were debates! Girls played sports — they could play tennis, and soccer! They could join music classes, and a drama club!

223

They were far behind for their age in most subjects, but they were thrilled. And so was I.

I tried to caution myself against too much joy. This was too good to last. It would all change when Yeslam decided to take us back to Jeddah, and returning home would be even harder for the girls after they had lived through such freedom. Still, inwardly, I was jubilant. In November, Mikhail Gorbachev and Ronald Reagan had a historical summit meeting in Switzerland. Our village, located just outside Geneva, bristled with army trucks, with multiple check-points on the road, and the threatening atmosphere panicked Yeslam. He said we should leave, that it was too dangerous to stay. I knew full well that our village was probably the safest place on the planet at that point, since the President of the United States was staying there, but there was no reasoning with Yeslam's alarm. He wanted us all to go to London for the summit's duration.

The children had just started school, I reasoned that it was unfair to pull them out so quickly. And I didn't want to establish a precedent, I so longed for them to spend one entire, blissful semester in Switzerland. So, to pacify Yeslam, who refused to take the plane on his own, I agreed to leave for London with him, and arranged for a tutor to come and look after the girls for a few days, along with my dear Dita, our faithful Filipina nanny.

It was only when I was seated in the plane that I realized that Yeslam, who was persuaded that our house was in danger, had nonetheless left the children there. I knew it was safe, but Yeslam believed that it wasn't. He had abandoned them. I turned and studied Yeslam as he sat beside me. The day we really are in danger, I thought, will Yeslam be the first to leave? Does he no longer care for anyone but himself?

Yeslam could still function, at least professionally. He already had a company with an office in Geneva. Now he began meeting the Saudi princes as they arrived in Geneva for vacations, cultivating them as friends and clients, becoming a kind of right-hand man. Yeslam knew people at the Saudi embassy and at Saudia, the national airline, and they kept him informed of who was scheduled to come to town. Yeslam would greet the Princes at the airport and spend afternoons and evenings with them.

Yeslam loved clothes and must have owned over three hundred suits, but now he went into overdrive. He developed a kind of competition with Prince Meshal as to who would be the most elegant. Yeslam always said King Fahd would pay any expense Prince

225

Meshal could incur, because Fahd wanted to keep Meshal out of the succession, despite his rank. By age, Meshal should be the successor to the Sultan, but Fahd had other plans for the Kingdom. This was the price King Fahd was willing to pay: he bought Meshal's birthright to take over the throne.

I was so thrilled at the children's progress in school. They were so happy, and as their first semester ended, their teachers informed us that they were catching up quickly with the curriculum. But I felt destitute and utterly overcome by Yeslam's erratic behaviour.

Little by little, I had begun to feel alone with my husband. Even when he was physically present, Yeslam seemed not to be emotionally engaged. Simple pleasures like watching the children play, swimming with them or reading, no longer held his interest. With me, Yeslam complained constantly of feeling unwell, and talked of little other than his ailments and his family problems. He seemed to feel well and sharp only in the company of the Saudi princes.

I was simply too exhausted to carry a whole family without help. I wanted to shake him out of this funk he was in, centred on himself and his ailments. I worried for him and I felt he needed professional help. I couldn't seem to help him. It's hard seeing someone complain of symptoms that seem imaginary. Often we would dress for an outing and begin driving into town only to stop and turn back because Yeslam couldn't face it.

Paradoxically, Yeslam was becoming more Saudi, now that we were in Europe. I don't know whether it was out of guilt that we had settled overseas. In Saudi Arabia, he and I had shared our bewilderment at Saudi society and socialized with Westerners. Now, living in a modern society, Yeslam sought out the company of other Saudi men, expectantly awaiting the arrival of the Princes. He seemed to need his roots, and with me and the children he became far more domineering.

Yeslam restricted our clothing — not too short, or bare — and our lifestyle. I was living in the free world now, but I found that I always had to be at his disposal. I never went out socially without him, and he even accompanied me to lunches with women friends. In a closed society, Yeslam gave me small freedoms, but now, in an open society, he clenched shut.

I don't know if it was the influence of the Saudi men he socialized with, but Yeslam began seeing other women. One spring day the phone rang. A man said, 'Tell your husband to stop running after my wife.' It was the husband of Yeslam's secretary. I was devastated. I had thought Yeslam was out late at night with the Princes. He didn't have many male friends, so when he went out without me I just assumed it was always for business. I realized he had been lying to me. I was shaken. Yeslam told me I was hysterical. At first he stonewalled, insisted he had done nothing. When I threatened to leave, he panicked. We made up, eventually, but something truly was wrong with our marriage.

I became pregnant once more. I knew that I would have this child, no matter what. This child was God-sent. When Yeslam dared to ask me to have another abortion, I felt disgust with him. How could he ask me to repeat that horrible procedure and its long, sad aftermath? Never, I told him. No matter what. Never again. With hindsight, I suppose this was when Yeslam finally felt I let him down. I went ahead with the pregnancy, though he had asked me not to. This was the end of my marriage: my refusal, his anger.

But perhaps the long, sad process that led to the end of my marriage had begun far earlier, in Saudi Arabia, when Yeslam's bold, Western personality began to crack and unravel. Perhaps it was the constant tension among the brothers, and their hidden struggle for money, power and prestige which undid my husband. After the Mecca revolt, nothing in Saudi Arabia was ever the same. It was then, I think, that the tensions between fundamentalist extremism and Western-generated ideas of material wealth became unbearable. Then Saudi Arabia began in some sense to realize that its culture was splitting into a modern economy and an ancient social code — contradictions that Saudi culture was unable or unwilling to resolve. Perhaps it was that tension that gnawed away at Yeslam, too.

Whatever the cause, whatever the moment when the wind finally shifted course — Yeslam had changed. All through my pregnancy, he barely spoke to me. He was cold, silent, forbidding. He would come back late, at three or four in the morning. My husband was truly a stranger to me then.

When the baby was born, I named her Noor, meaning the light. And she was indeed my light, later, when the world around me sometimes seemed so dark. Even just hours old, Noor was so lovely, with her huge open eyes — not wrinkled and red like most babies, but calm, from the beginning, and clear-sighted.

Yeslam made efforts to be attentive after Noor's birth. He was affectionate with her, and even with me. He insisted I return home from the clinic early, and I did. I had to leave Noor there because she had a mild case of jaundice. Yeslam accompanied me to the clinic at least once a day to feed her. Part of me tried to persuade myself that Yeslam was happy, but more likely he already knew, then, that everything would be over soon. More likely he was happy because he had someone else. I understood that something had been broken between us, but I didn't know what to do to make it mend. I spent hours on the phone to Mary Martha, seeking comfort.

Noor was born in April 1987. In September, I saw Yeslam with another woman. I hadn't been able to sleep that night, and as I often did, I went out for a drive around town. (For some reason automobiles have always soothed me.) I happened to drive past Yeslam's offices and I caught sight of his car. So I parked and waited. It was about one in the morning when Yeslam walked out, with a woman.

I confronted him. Yeslam denied that he knew the woman, but he was obviously lying. I knew I should leave him now, but I couldn't bear to hurt the children. Above all, I feared that he would try to take them away from me and back to Saudi Arabia. I was exhausted and depressed, worn out by Noor's birth and the loneliness of my pregnancy and I couldn't

230

face the battle that I knew lay ahead.

Meanwhile, Yeslam had begun pressuring me to sign a legal agreement. It was a sort of pre-nuptial agreement, except that it was post-nuptial. Yeslam told me it was a formality, to protect the children's security. My doctor advised me that I was in no fit state to make any major decisions, but when I hesitated, Yeslam became grimmer than I had ever seen him.

'Look, I didn't want Noor, and you went ahead anyway,' he told me. 'If you don't want problems, if you want me to accept her, you'll trust me, and you'll sign it.'

I was a wreck, physically and mentally. Yeslam threatened me. He said, again and again, that he would take the girls to Jeddah and leave them with his mother. I could not bear his constant pressure. I knew that under Swiss law Yeslam would be allowed to take the children on vacation, alone. And I knew that if the children ever set foot in Saudi Arabia, I would never see them again. No government on earth would ever get them out.

I felt trapped by my own husband. The only thing that mattered to me was that he would not take my daughters away from me. At my wit's end, and in a state of panic, I gave in and signed the paper. More than anything, I needed to end Yeslam's harassment.

Things only got worse after I signed the document, though. Yeslam didn't change, as I had hoped he would. He became increasingly distant, and was rarely at home. My own health worsened. I couldn't eat and began losing weight. I could barely look after the children. I was hospitalized for a few days in October, hooked up to intravenous feeding tubes. I weighed 99 pounds.

That Christmas, struggling to maintain a semblance of normal family life for the girls, I took baby Noor and the children to the mountains. Yeslam was supposed to meet us there, but he called and said that Prince Meshal was in town. Part of me wanted to believe him, but I knew he was lying.

On New Year's night, Yeslam went out, but came home early. He fell asleep — we had begun sleeping in separate bedrooms. The phone kept ringing, but every time I answered the caller hung up. I woke him, told him I thought someone was trying to call. The next morning he went out early and came back claiming it had probably all been a stupid, drunken New Year's joke. I was vulnerable, but I was not an imbecile. I might have reacted differently if Yeslam had been honest with me, but I couldn't accept such

232

blatant lies. We had an argument. Yeslam was livid. I asked him to leave. He slammed the door on his way out. So, on New Year's Day of 1988, my life changed.

What followed was bitter and draining, and I see little benefit in dwelling on it. The girls and I remained in Switzerland. The Bin Laden family rejected them completely. Once, I went to visit Yeslam's brother Ibrahim, who had been my friend, and pleaded for him to intercede with Yeslam, but he told me, 'No matter how right you are, Carmen, my brother is never wrong.'

Another time, Najia caught sight of Om Yeslam, her grandmother, and Fawzia, her aunt, on a street in Geneva. These women turned away from my little girl, who had grown up in their company. None of the Bin Ladens, even those who seemed to enjoy my company, ever had the strength of mind to stand up to Yeslam and contact me or my children.

Our divorce procedure has been appalling. Yeslam has poured all his might and money into a colossal effort to keep me under his control, and exact his revenge. Although he had promised not to, he demanded the right to take Noor to Saudi Arabia, though not Wafah and Najia, I suppose because he thought the older children could refuse. He fought every detail tooth and nail, and dragged the legal battle out over the longest possible time, so that he could hide his assets and deprive the children and myself of his financial support.

Perhaps the worst moment of our long story together came after I was granted custody of the children. That's when Yeslam claimed that he was not Noor's father. It was unspeakably low of him, and utterly humiliating to me, and, above all, to little Noor. It's hard to see how anyone could do such a thing. His claim was of course false, as we proved.

I had to ask that all of us go through DNA tests to confirm that Yeslam was lying, and that Noor really is her father's child. She was just nine years old. Yeslam walked into the clinic while Noor and I were in the doctor's office. Wafah sprang at him, and asked how he could do something like that. Yeslam just ignored her. He walked straight past his daughters. From that day on, Yeslam never spoke again to any of his daughters, or to me.

The whole battle continues to this day. We are legally separated. Wafah and Najia are legally adults and Noor is safe in my custody. I attempt to support us all on alimony payments allotted to me by a Swiss court, which amounts to less than the monthly salary of Yeslam's private pilot. Sometimes I feel like David, to Yeslam's Goliath.

If we had been in Saudi Arabia, the divorce would have been so simple for Yeslam. It would have been over in less than half a day, and I would have lost my children for ever. But we were in Switzerland, and one man believed in the threat that hung over my daughters — my Swiss lawyer, Frédéric Marti.

Yeslam lives in Geneva now, as I do. When he sees his daughters, he stares right through them. He refuses any contact with them whatsoever, and when Wafah was accepted by Columbia law school in New York, he said he would never support her because there was no point in her studying more.

Yeslam asked for Swiss nationality in the late 1990s, which provoked great controversy in Switzerland. But early in 2001 obtaining a Swiss passport seemed suddenly to become very important and urgent to him. So he staged an elaborate media campaign, claiming that he needed to be sure he could live in Switzerland in order to stay close to his children, even though he had completely cut off contact with them for many years. I cannot help thinking he used our children to further his interests. However, in May 2001, Yeslam was rewarded with his Swiss passport.

Whatever his nationality, Yeslam is truly a Saudi.

He has ceaselessly harassed us with legal procedures. Twice I received frightening official letters from Saudi Arabia demanding that I appear before a court of law in Jeddah. When my lawyer asked for an explanation, Yeslam claimed that this was for a Saudi divorce. I knew that he was lying because, under shariah law, a Saudi divorce doesn't require the presence of the wife. I believe that Yeslam charged me with adultery. In Saudi Arabia, the sentence for that would be death.

If he has charged me with adultery, as I believe he has, then Yeslam has cut me off not only from Saudi Arabia but from the entire Middle East. I am afraid to set foot in any Muslim countries which have close legal ties with Saudi Arabia for I could be extradited, and I would be at the mercy of a legal system that would be prepared to carry out a death sentence on an innocent woman. I fear for my life.

I have come to believe that dealing with my unbelievably lengthy divorce is the price that I will have to pay for my daughter's freedom. Although it has been a long and bitter fight, it is not such a very high price to pay for the precious knowledge that my three girls can now live as they wish.

Yeslam's rejection of our daughters hurt them enormously as they grew up, and they still pay a heavy emotional price. Rejection, especially from a father, is a very hard thing for a little girl to have to bear. A father's admiration and love is so important. I know a little of what it is like. I felt that awful grief and guilt myself, when my own father left us. I, too, suffered, as have my daughters; I, too, felt myself painfully to blame. It is a terrible thing to watch this happen to my children.

I wonder, now, if Yeslam cut off his daughters because Saudi values are foreign to them. They are intelligent, educated, beautiful, lively and graceful, and they are free women. But perhaps he only really sees them as pawns, tools that he can use against me. Or maybe as enemies. Perhaps to him they seem unworthy of his attention because they are Western women, wilful and independent. Or is it because they are mine, and we must be enemies now?

My struggle to keep my daughters has made me stronger. But it seems to me that Yeslam has changed far more than I have. Or perhaps at some deeper level, my husband was always a Saudi: self-centred, arrogant and dismissive. His background simply caught up with him as he grew older. I was blind to reality, star-struck and foolish, imagining a love-story where there was only a struggle for power and dominance. Once I disobeyed, my dream turned to dust, and my charming prince turned against me: it was all a Saudi fairy tale, and the brunt of my punishment will always be borne by my children.

Wafah and Najia are adults now. Noor is getting older too. We have decided to keep our name — Yeslam's name. Whatever has happened between us, Yeslam remains my children's father. And our name is Bin Ladin. Once, it was a name like any other. Today it has become a synonym of blind violence, and terror. We could of course try to change our name, but my daughters and I have nothing to hide, and we do not want to mislead anyone. The truth always catches up with you one day, and changing our name would not change who we are. If my daughters go back to Saudi Arabia one day, it will be their free choice, as, long ago, it was mine. But, as a mother, I hope with every fibre of my body they never do.

Conclusion

For many people, September 11 2001 marked the start of a new era. It was a wake-up call. That day opened the eyes of the West to a vast and powerful latent menace of which few had been aware. For the first time, the Western world had to measure the power of Islamic fundamentalism to rock its foundations. Osama Bin Laden and his followers were able to take our freedom hostage. The attack robbed us all of a certain innocence.

I have lived in the Bin Laden clan and experienced the workings of Saudi society, and I fear for the future of the free world. My fear and outrage is based on my conviction that a large majority of Saudis support the extremist ideas of Osama Bin Laden, and that the Bin Ladens and the Saudi royal family continue to operate hand in hand, even if their relations are sometimes too intricate for their convergent convictions to be apparent.

The Bin Ladens have never said they have rejected Osama completely. Would they deprive him of his share and divide it among themselves? Under shariah law that could

239

only be done for a recognized religious offence. The Bin Ladens and the princes work together, very closely. They are secretive, and they are united. They have been inextricably linked for many decades through close friendships and business ventures. Most of the Bin Laden brothers have business partnerships and direct vested interests with at least one Saudi prince. For example, Bakr Bin Laden is a business associate of Abdel Aziz Ben Fahd, the King's preferred son, and Yeslam Bin Ladin has privileged links with Prince Meshal Ben Abdel Aziz.

Both clans have disassociated themselves from Osama Bin Laden and the barbaric acts that led to Nine Eleven. They have made strong public statements condemning the attacks, describing the killing of innocent people as being in contradiction of Islamic faith, and said they have no connections with Osama Bin Laden's works or activities, but what are they doing actively to prevent the spread of terror?

I openly defy the Saudi ruling class — the Bin Ladens and the Saudi royal family — to open their books and prove to the world where they stand. In the current precarious political climate, no one can afford to hide behind the weak excuse of privacy. I believe it is the duty of each and every one of us to do everything in our power in the fight against terrorism. These are people who feel contempt for the outside world. Individually, some of them may claim to be liberal, but the beliefs and ideology of their culture are deeply ingrained in them from an early age.

Saudis don't openly argue with each other. Sometimes the thirst for power, greed and material interests might cause rifts among the brothers within a family like the al-Sauds or the Bin Ladens, but they will always be kept together by the bonds of their shared beliefs, religious convictions and their upbringing.

Osama Bin Laden and those like him didn't spring, fully formed, from the desert sand. They were made. They were fashioned by the workings of an opaque and intolerant medieval society which is closed to the outside world. It is a society where half the population have had their basic human rights denied to them and obedience to the strictest rules of Islam must be absolute. When Osama dies, I fear there will be a thousand men to take his place.

Despite all the power of their oil revenue, the Saudis are structured by a hateful, backwards-looking view of religion, and an education that is a school for intolerance. They learn scorn for what is foreign: the non-Muslim doesn't count. Their mothers spoil them into arrogance, but then their every natural instinct is denied by endless, oppressive restrictions. Obedience to the patriarch is absolute. And when they become fathers, their rule is law.

I have never yet met a Saudi who truly admires our Western society, though they are eager to use our technology and they understand our political systems. But inside them, there is nothing but scorn for what they perceive as the godless, individualistic values and shameless freedoms of the Western way of life.

And yet, in Saudi Arabia there is much drug abuse and promiscuity, homosexuality and AIDS. There is certainly much more hypocrisy than anywhere in the West where I have ever been. But these things are not openly displayed or honestly discussed. For the Saudis, it seems, what is hidden does not exist.

There must be geniuses lost in that people. Osama, perhaps, could have been one. But, though he lived in the twenty-first century, he did not use his influence and power to bring people closer together, to promote good will and tolerance. Instead, he chose discord and destruction.

In the end I believe that Osama was shaped by the strict doctrine of Wahhabism. In my analysis and experience, a vast majority of people in Saudi Arabia feel just like him. In their eyes, you cannot be too religious. They have no room to grow as individuals. They are desperately angry at the West for its countless, irresistible temptations. They refuse to evolve or to adapt. For them, it is easier to crush those temptations and destroy them. I hope I am wrong but, unfortunately, I believe that the fundamentalists who are at the receiving end of Saudi Arabia's oil wealth are here to stay. I fear that if we, in the Western world, are not vigilant enough, there will be no end to their terrorism. They will use our tolerance to infiltrate our society with their intolerance.

In those long years I spent in Saudi Arabia, and the years of struggle that followed, I fought to stay true to myself and to give my daughters what is priceless: freedom of thought. I hope I made the right choice. I don't know if that's as important to them as it is to me. I suppose that when I was younger, I, too, found it less important. But when I felt it was being taken away from me and feared that it might slip out of my grasp, I found that was the one thing I could not tolerate.

I have seen too many women lose everything, even the right to see their children, and who were forced to submit to the rule of their husbands because they simply had no other choice. I have seen men torn between their ambition and desires, and their training for self-denial and obedience to their society's traditions.

Sometimes I wonder whether I would have fought the Bin Laden clan less fiercely if I had had only sons. Materially, it was in many ways a pleasant existence, but as much as material things tempt me, there are other things that matter far more.

I am aware that because I dare to speak up, a war will be declared on my daughters and me by the powerful Bin Laden clan and the Saudi establishment. Lawsuits will be filed, our integrity questioned, our credibility discredited. To them it is a crime for us, as women, to aspire to freedom of thought and the protection of our basic rights as human beings.

But we will fight back. Our defence is the defence of truth. Our serenity, our well-being, our most basic sense of security was shattered and buried on September 11 2001. Now, more than ever, is the time for us to speak up and rise above the lies and duplicity that made the tragedy possible, to try to protect our future.

Despite everything we have gone through and no matter what the future holds for us, I want my daughters to know that I will never regret saying yes to their father. As a young girl, I accepted him and loved him madly. Unfortunately, I found that as a mother and a woman, I could not accept the beliefs and values which were such an important part of him. I want my daughters to know that I am convinced, deep in my heart and conscience, that by giving them my values, I gave them the most valuable gift of all — freedom. For me, there will never be a better reward than to be able to look at my beautiful daughters and say, 'Wafah, Najia and Noor, you are free to live the lives you want to live, and, above all, you are free to be who you want to be.'

We do hope that you have enjoyed reading this large print book.

Did you know that all of our titles are available for purchase?

We publish a wide range of high quality large print books including:
Romances, Mysteries, Classics
General Fiction
Non Fiction and Westerns

Special interest titles available in large print are:
The Little Oxford Dictionary
Music Book
Song Book
Hymn Book
Service Book

Also available from us courtesy of Oxford University Press:
Young Readers' Dictionary
(large print edition)
Young Readers' Thesaurus
(large print edition)

For further information or a free brochure, please contact us at:
Ulverscroft Large Print Books Ltd.,
The Green, Bradgate Road, Anstey,
Leicester, LE7 7FU, England.
Tel: (00 44) 0116 236 4325
Fax: (00 44) 0116 234 0205

Other titles published by
The House of Ulverscroft:

CARRION KISSES

Kate Lock

Exeter University, 1981: When naive undergraduate Kate meets charismatic mature student Tim Franklin, recently released from prison on a life sentence, he takes her over completely. Their explosive affair, which began so passionately, ends in vicious emotional cruelty, but it's not until Tim dies that Kate discovers the extremes he was capable of. Twenty years on, she uncovers a trail of Machiavellian deception that leaves her questioning everything she once knew about the man — including her own role in the relationship.

BURNED ALIVE

Souad
in collaboration with
Marie-Thérèse Cuny

When Souad was seventeen she fell in love. In her village, as in so many others, sex before marriage was considered a grave dishonour to one's family and was punishable by death. This was her crime. Her brother-in-law was given the task of arranging her punishment. One morning, he crept up on her, poured petrol over her and set her alight. In the eyes of their community he was a hero. Miraculously, Souad survived, rescued by the women of the village. She has now decided to tell her story and uncover the barbarity of honour killings, a practice which still continues.

DRIFTING WITH THE RIVER GODS

Martin Quigley

Rivers run through all our lives and are magnets for young boys. From an early age, The Boy lived with his Uncle Paddy, who was an expert boatman and fisherman. He introduced The Boy to life, and to trout and salmon angling on the River Suir. Thus began a lifelong devotion to waterways. We accompany The Boy on his personal journey, sharing his experiences and speculations. We see the world through his eyes during one idyllic 1960s Irish summer, when he finds happiness but also meets despair. Packed with colourful characters, adventure, mischief and humour, yet tinged with sadness, this is a soulful and reflective insight into nature and people.

BEST FOOT FORWARD

Susie Kelly

Why would an unfit, fifty-something Englishwoman embark on a solo walk across France from La Rochelle on the west coast to Lake Geneva over the Swiss border? With no experience of hiking or camping, Susie Kelly found out the hard way that it is possible to be overloaded and ill-prepared at the same time. Scorching days, glacial nights, perpetual blisters, inaccurate maps, a leaking tent and an inappropriate sleeping bag were daily vexations, but as she hobbled eastwards, the glory of the French landscape revealed its magic and the kindness of strangers repaid her discomfort in spades.

THE KEEPER OF ABSALOM'S ISLAND

Tom Nestor

For Tom Nestor, childhood was a soaring adventure across a rural landscape. With no place for him on the land or affinity with its toils, he resolves to escape. With his pack of dogs he strides off into the carefree world of a curious boy in a magical time. Set in the countryside around Rathkeale in County Limerick, not twenty miles from the poverty-stricken lanes and ashes of Limerick city, this memoir is peopled with such characters as the mad aristocratic Absalom Creagh, and Miss James and Miss Abigail who taught through the medium of religion and terror.

SCOTTISH SPECTRES

Dane Love

Here is a ghoulish collection of over two hundred hauntings from the length and breadth of Scotland. Whilst castles, old inns and pubs are the usual residences of spirits, there are sightings of spectres at some rather more unusual locations such as hospitals, ships, lighthouses, supermarkets, theatres, coalmines, restaurants, and even toilets! There is the ghostly presence of a surgeon who haunts the hospital where he once worked, the disruptive poltergeist at a supermarket, the restaurant which echoes to the sounds of long-forgotten children, and a prison frequented by the spirit of a hanged man who suffered a most gruesome death — and much, much more.

I spent the rest of the week alone. I saw no one. I spoke to no one. I lived with my thoughts, and in the silence I tried to come to terms with all that I had learned.

On Friday night, I went to the Bear. Dave Evans was working the bar. I had already told him by phone that I was done with the job, and he had taken it well. I guess he knew that it would only be a matter of time. I had already received unofficial confirmation that my PI's license would be restored to me within days, just as Epstein had told me, and all objections to my license to carry had been withdrawn.

But that night, it was clear that Dave was swamped. The main bar area was jammed, so it was standing room only. I stepped aside to let Sarah pass by with a tray of beer orders in one hand, a stack of food orders in the other. She looked frazzled, which was unusual, but then I noticed that everybody else who was working did too.

'Gary Maser gave me twenty-four hours' notice, then left,' said Dave, as he juggled mixing a brandy Alexander with keeping an eye on three pints that were pouring simultaneously. 'Pity. I liked him. I figured he might stay on. Any idea what happened there?'

'None,' I said.

'Well, you hired him.'